Bike Paths

OF CONNECTICUT

Bike Paths

OF CONNECTICUT

A Guide to Rail-Trails & Other Car-Free Places

by Stuart Johnstone

photographs by the author

Active
PUBLICATIONS

www.activepublications.net

Send your comments!
Conditions and information change over time so we appreciate hearing corrections which you find. Opinions and suggestions are also welcome. Address them to:

Active Publications
P.O. Box 1037
Concord, MA 01742-1037

Published by:
    Active Publications
    P.O. Box 1037
    Concord, MA 01742-1037

    www.activepublications.net

Printed in the United States of America

Publisher's Cataloging in Publication Data

Johnstone, Stuart A.
    Bike Paths of Connecticut: A Guide to Rail-Trails and Other Car-Free Places / by Stuart A. Johnstone; photographs by the author.
    ISBN 0-9627990-9-2
    1. Bicycle touring - Connecticut - Guidebooks 2. Connecticut - Description and travel
    Library of Congress Catalog Card Number: 2001 129068

This book is dedicated to the many forms of human-powered travel, and to the people and places that inspire it.

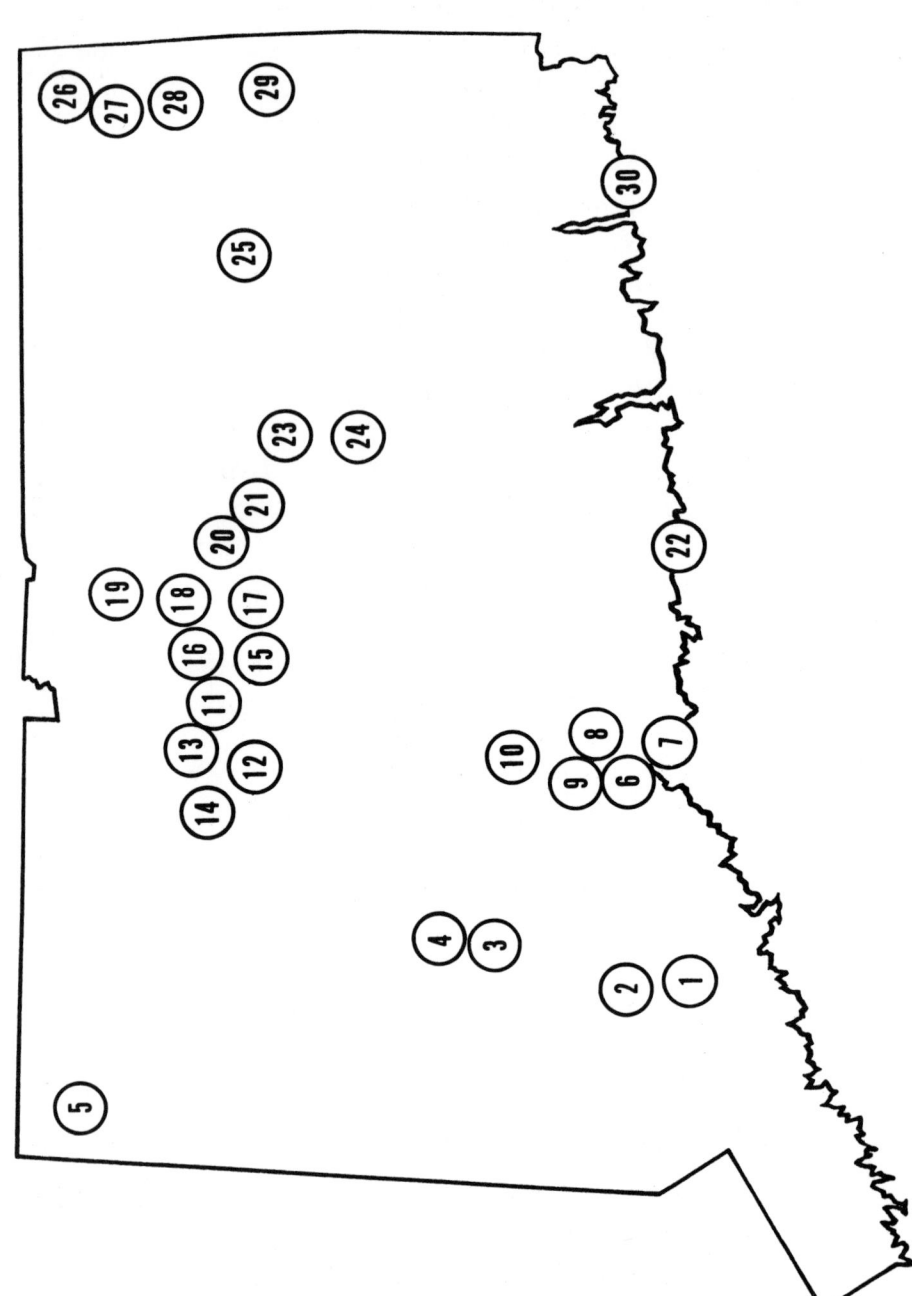

Contents

Introduction

Bike Paths of Connecticut

A bike path is a precious thing. Separated from the hazards, noise, and exhaust fumes of public roadways, a bike path is able to deliver much more than the people which it carries. Travel a trail and you are apt to feel free from the hustle of everyday life, to appreciate and enjoy your exercise, to notice the nature around you, and to say hello to strangers as they pass. The atmosphere is safe, calming, and fun-filled.

Connecticut's diverse and growing network of bike paths, both paved and unpaved, is an increasingly popular resource for recreation and transportation. The options include convenient locations in or near urban centers as well as the rural settings of vacation destinations, protected natural areas, and historic sites. Many are flat, easy routes along former railroads which are now linear parklands linking distant towns while others take free-flowing courses through a variety of landscapes in state parks and other public lands. The most popular paths attract steady streams of human-powered traffic but others venture into remote woodlands with plenty of peace and quiet. Wherever they lie, the bike paths of Connecticut are havens for exercising, relaxing, and commuting in the great outdoors.

Bike Paths of Connecticut has been written from the bicyclist's perspective but in-line skaters, walkers, and runners will find the trail descriptions and directions equally useful. A primary objective of the book is to communicate rules and regulations, standards of etiquette, and safety features for the state's many trails since each location has its own set of conditions. By providing this information it is hoped that readers will gain an appreciation for the diversity of Connecticut's greenways and be able to plan their rides accordingly.

Variety of Bike Paths

Connecticut's bike paths reflect the state's diverse landscape. Some serve multitudes of people in urban areas and others explore rural locations with barely a soul to be seen. Hilly, flat, long, or short, most paved trails are classified in the following three groups:

Rail-trails include some of the state's most popular bike paths. Guided by the nationwide efforts of the Rails-to-Trails Conservancy, the conversion of unused railroad corridors to recreational trails has established miles of level, car-free routes which conveniently join distant locations. These "linear parks" are managed either by local authorities or the state's Department of Environmental Protection.

State parks and forests are the responsibility of the Department of Environmental Protection (D.E.P.) and offer a number of multi-use trails for passive recreation. Winding through forests and over small hills, many of these bike paths enjoy undisturbed, natural scenery.

Local bike paths follow roadsides, conservation lands, and other areas belonging to a town or community. They vary widely in scenery and are often among the least publicized routes.

Many of the state's bike paths date from the 1980's and '90's when interest in bicycling, running, and other forms of outdoor exercise increased. As roads have became more crowded with traffic, separated bike paths have become more popular and community, state, and federal government initiatives have reflected the importance of being able to travel without cars and of having safe places to exercise and recreate.

Bike paths continue to be planned throughout the state in order to satisfy growing public interest. Future bike paths have been proposed in many locations extending existing routes and establishing entirely new ones. Since

4

creating new bike paths requires public support and years of planning, volunteers and interested individuals are urged to get involved and contribute what they can. Contact the Connecticut Bicycle Coalition (1 Union Place, Hartford, CT 06103, Tel. (860) 527-5200, or www.ctbike.org) to learn about bike path projects in your area.

Closed to cars and open only to passive recreation, Connecticut's bike paths inspire a variety of human-powered activity:

Bicycling continues to have increasing appeal thanks to its smooth, low-impact motion and long-range mobility. Kids, young adults, parents, and elders all have their own reasons for riding but agree on the value of pedaling in safe, natural settings that are separated from the traffic, noise, and exhaust fumes of the roads.

In-line skating, one of the country's fastest-growing sports, has found a welcome home on many of the state's paved trails. Free to focus their attention on the scenery rather than the passing cars, in-line skaters can smoothly roll for long distances on rail-trails and other paved pathways.

Walking and **running** are the most popular means of travel on some paths. Many pedestrians prefer to be off the roads but do not feel comfortable exploring the woods on hiking trails, so smooth-surfaced bike paths are the ideal middle ground providing safe, peaceful conditions for a walk, jog, or a stroll with a carriage or wheelchair.

Rules of the Bike Path

Some of Connecticut's bike paths attract many visitors and a variety of activities. During the busiest periods they are alive with people of different ages, people doing different activities, and people traveling at different speeds, so it is important that everyone follow the same set of rules.

The following is a list of general guidelines for use of a bike path:

1. **Keep to the right.** Most bike paths have two-way traffic so keep to the right side to allow safe passage. Remember that others might need to pass you.

2. **Pass on the left after giving an audible signal.** Make verbal contact ("-on your left") or signal with a bell to avoid startling the slower traveler. Look both ahead and behind before passing.

3. **Yield to pedestrians and horseback riders.** Walkers, runners, and horseback riders have the right-of-way at all times. Bicyclists, in-line skaters, and others must yield.

4. **Stop at road crossings and look both ways.** Drivers will not always be aware of bike path crossings so assume that they do not see you.

5. **Stay alert and be predictable.** Anticipate the actions of others and let them anticipate yours by avoiding sudden changes in movement.

6. **Do not block the bike path when stopped.** Step off the surface to allow others to pass unimpeded.

Connecticut law requires children under age 12 to wear an approved helmet when operating a bicycle or being carried as a passenger on a bicycle on public roads and bike paths.

Serious injuries are possible on bike paths even with only a few people present. Bicyclists and in-line skaters pose an especially high risk for accidents since they travel relatively quickly and quietly. Crowded conditions, road crossings, and the presence of children and pets increase the amount of risk.

Bike paths are not meant for speed. Bicyclists and in-line skaters planning on fast speeds should either use the roads or take special care in choosing an appropriate place and time to ride.

Noise and litter have a negative impact for other bike path users and for abutting property owners. Respect the environment of the trail so that others can enjoy it too.

Pet owners should know local leash laws and be aware of rules regarding animal wastes. At many parks and greenways, owners are required to remove their pet's wastes and dispose of them according to certain regulations.

All areas ask that visitors not block trailhead gates when parking because work crews and emergency vehicles always need access. Park at designated public locations.

Planning Your Trip

Be prepared! Getting lost or injured, underestimating trip length or difficulty, and overestimating your own strength or skill level can bring undesireable consequences. A weather change or equipment failure can ruin an otherwise wonderful time. Be ready for unwanted surprises by planning ahead and bringing some useful items.

Drinking water is one of the most essential things to remember, especially in summer. It is easy to become dehydrated while exercising so carry a water bottle or two on the bike frame or in a fanny pack and start drinking before you get thirsty. Many of the longer tours described in this book could require greater amounts. Remember that water taken from streams should be considered unsafe since it often harbors infectious bacteria such as Giardia lamblia, spread when human and animal wastes are deposited near water sources. Be careful not to contribute to the problem.

Even if you are not planning a picnic, bring along something to eat on longer excursions in case your body runs low on fuel. A high-energy snack can give an important boost both physically and psychologically.

If you are unsure of the trails that you plan to explore, carry a map and keep track of the features that you pass such as road crossings, bridges, and bodies of water. Bicyclists can follow the mileage directions for bike paths with cyclometers, tiny trip computers which mount on the handlebars to display distance, time, speed, and other helpful information.

Bicyclists should consider bringing tools for simple repairs. Since many of the paths described in this book visit isolated places, riders should be able to fix a flat tire or repair a simple mechanical failure. Common supplies include either a spare inner tube or a patch kit, a pump, tire irons to remove the tire from the rim, a set of wrenches and screw drivers to tighten or adjust various parts, a spoke wrench, and chain tool. These items can be carried in a small bike pack fitted to the bike. If you are not capable of making general repairs on the trail and are not self-sufficient with tools, ride with others who are.

Other useful items include bug repellent during spring and summer when mosquitoes, deer flies, and other insects can create unwanted memories, and extra clothing and rain gear for longer journeys since weather changes can occur suddenly. First-aid supplies are also wise. These items add minimal amounts of weight relative to their potential reward.

Finally, travel with a companion and leave word of your destination with a responsible person. Some readers might not feel comfortable traveling alone on bike paths in either the urban or rural locations described in this book.

What to Wear

If you are traveling on wheels, the most important item is a helmet. Light in weight and comfortable to wear, it should be worn by all ages as valuable protection from the pavement, trees, and other people encountered along the way. Connecticut law requires that children age 12 and under wear a helmet when riding a bicycle or when being

transported by a bicycle on a public road or bike path. Since three quarters of all bicycle deaths result from head injuries, wearing a helmet is a healthy habit. In-line skaters are also encouraged to wear knee, elbow, and wrist protection.

Nearly anything will do for clothes, but dress in layers to allow your body time to warm up and to suit possible weather changes. Wear comfortable clothing that has been tried and tested and is meant for the activity that you are planning. Bike shorts are especially recommended for cyclists because the elastic material fits close to the body to eliminate chafing and the padded crotch provides a welcome cushion.

About this Guidebook

Bike Paths of Connecticut is meant to be a starting point, a means for people to discover a new place for themselves. It has been written to prepare readers with information on rules and regulations, trail descriptions, background information, and suggested destinations so that they can better enjoy their explorations. Narrated directions are provided but should be recognized as only one of perhaps several ways to tour an area.

Maps are included to give a general view of trail networks and natural features. Note that the map scale for each area varies widely so plan your distances and courses carefully. The names of trails, roads, and surrounding landmarks appear in boldface in the text for quick referencing. Only the major parking areas are illustrated so smaller spots might also exist.

Practical information accompanies each description. This includes a listing of nearby bicycle shops for access to parts and repair services, the location of public toilet facilities, and sources for additional information. Driving directions from nearby highways are included and will be most helpful when used together with a road map.

Disclaimer

The author and Active Publications bear no liability for accidents, injuries, losses, or damages caused directly or indirectly by people engaged in the activities described in this book.

Bike Paths

OF CONNECTICUT

A Guide to Rail-Trails and Other Car-Free Places

1
Housatonic Rail Bed
Trumbull

length: 4.7 miles
surface: unpaved, with wet spots and a rough detour
terrain: flat

Trumbull's surprisingly secluded rail-trail remains relatively unimproved but its dramatic route along the steep, ledgy banks of the Pequonnock River draws a steady stream of admirers. The trail's mostly flat, trouble-free riding makes it easy for cyclists to soak up the great natural scenery.

BACKGROUND:
The route originated in 1840 as the Berkshire Railroad linking Bridgeport and New Milford, then was purchased by the Housatonic Railroad, and eventually became part of the New York, New Haven, and Hartford Railroad. Use of this segment of the rail line declined during the Great Depression and it was abandoned in 1941.

The Bridgeport Hydraulic Company owned and managed much of the surrounding acreage as watershed land from the 1880's until 1989 and prohibited any access to the area. Today the state of Connecticut owns the land, known as Pequonnock River Valley Park, and manages it in partnership with the town of Trumbull for recreation and conservation. The Housatonic Rail Bed serves as the park's main trail, a highlight for many visitors and merely a starting point for others eager to explore the area's more challenging hiking and mountain biking opportunities.

RULES OF THE TRAIL
Bicyclists are specifically asked to be alert and courteous to others, to yield the trail to walkers and horseback riders, and to ride on open trails only. Travel at a safe speed and warn walkers of your approach to avoid

startling them.

Hunting is permitted on parts of the state land from the third Saturday in October through the third Saturday of December on Mondays, Wednesdays, Fridays, and Saturdays. Dogs must be leashed at all times. The park closes at sunset.

ORIENTATION:

The Housatonic Rail Bed (also known as West Tr.) runs in a mostly north-south direction along the Pequonnock River. The smoothest, most popular part of the trail is the 2.7-mile stretch from Tait Rd. (at the southern endpoint) to Whitney Ave. Parking lots at both roads also make this the most accessible portion.

North of Whitney Ave., conditions are generally rougher and trail usage is less frequent. A detour from the original rail bed at Rte. 25 involves difficult biking conditions on a narrow and rocky path but is well marked by signs. Beyond Rte. 111, the trail surface is bumpy from tree roots and made narrow by encroaching foliage.

TRAIL DESCRIPTION:

Starting from **Tait Rd.** at the southern trailhead for **Pequonnock River Valley Park**, the first half-mile of the rail bed passes between two residential neighborhoods with small footpaths branching toward many of the back yards. It then enters natural surroundings and follows a shelf of land along a steep slope with the Pequonnock River visible and audible below the trail on the right side. The river and its rapids are a captivating sight along this stretch especially where narrow points in the valley constrict the flow to rocky chasms.

The trail continues northward with a faint uphill grade, curving with the shape of the hillside and leaving sight of the river at numerous points. Wet spots on the trail surface slow the pedaling but the biking is otherwise smooth. Intersecting side trails branch to the right, drop to the river, and connect Pequonnock River Valley Park's other trails.

About 1.3 miles from Tait Rd., look on the right for the

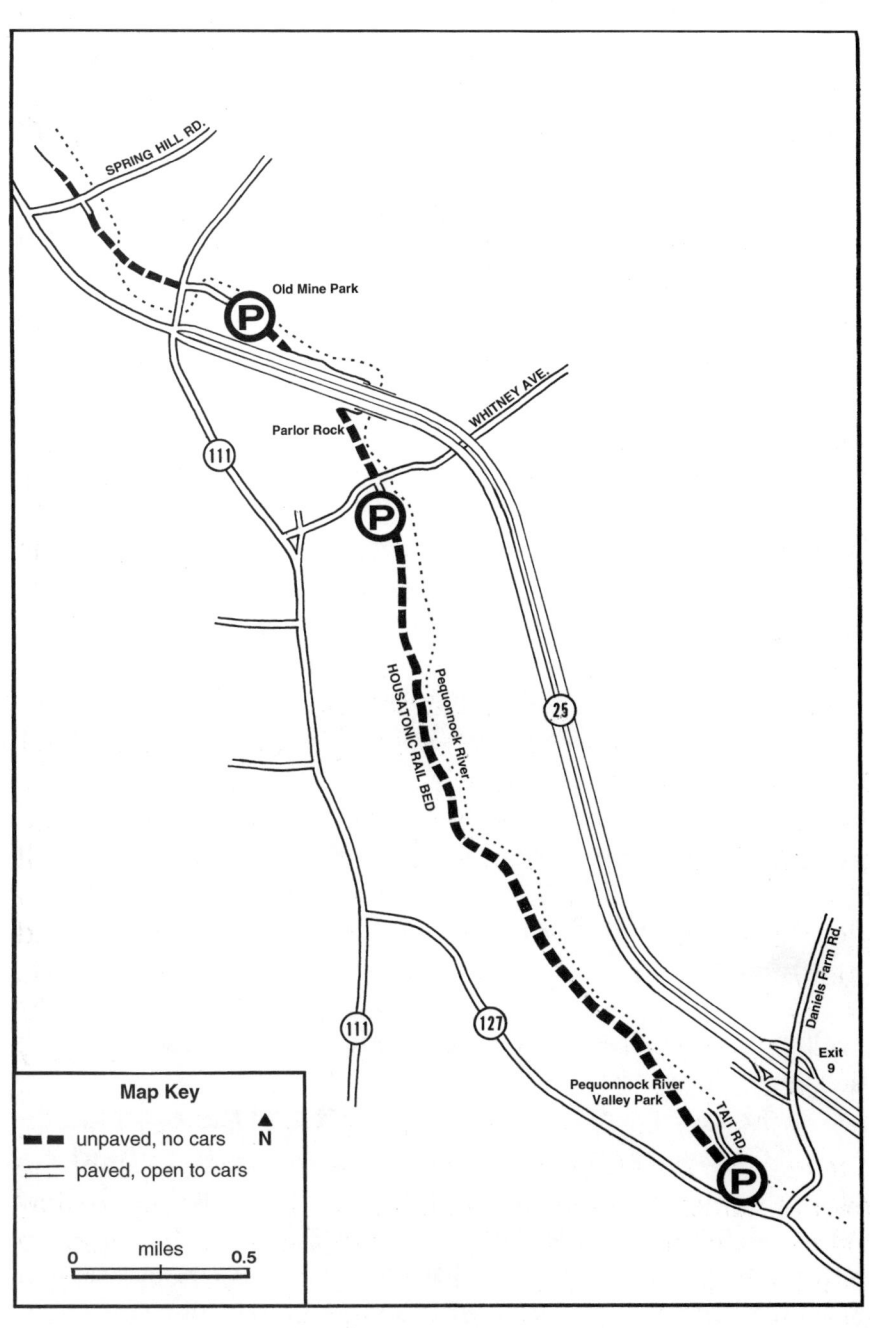

SPRING HILL RD.

Old Mine Park

WHITNEY AVE.

Parlor Rock

111

25

Pequonnock River

HOUSATONIC RAIL BED

111

127

Pequonnock River
Valley Park

TAIT RD.

Daniels Farm Rd.

Exit
9

Map Key

▲
N

━ ━ unpaved, no cars

─── paved, open to cars

miles

0   0.5

stone foundation of the Old Trumbull Ice House, built to store ice before the days of refrigeration. In winter, ice was harvested beside this building from a huge reservoir which also provided water for Bridgeport in the 1800's and early 1900's.

After 2.3 miles the trail narrows from overgrowing foliage in a semi-open area, passes a residence on the right, and at the 2.7-mile mark emerges at a trailhead parking lot on **Whitney Ave.** Here the easiest riding ends and bicyclists looking for smooth, firm conditions should reverse direction.

The rail bed crosses Whitney Ave. at a steep, blind corner so use caution when continuing northward. The trail surface is noticeably bumpier over the next quarter-mile to **Parlor Rock**, site of a late-1800's amusement park which was built by the railroad to attract passengers. A set of prominent ledges and a small gorge in the river make it a worthwhile resting point.

A 0.3-mile detour from the rail bed begins nearby where **Rte. 25** obstructs the original course. Marked by signs, the detour follows a rough, narrow footpath which can be ridden by skilled mountain bikers but should be walked by others. The path crosses beneath the roadway at a bridge spanning the Pequonnock River.

Soon after returning to the rail bed on the north side of Rte. 25, the trail arrives at **Old Mine Park** where a trailhead parking lot, small pond, and picnic area await. Owned by the town of Trumbull, this park was the site of an 1800's-era tungsten mine and remnants of the operation are still visible from the trails that explore the acreage.

Follow the park's driveway to **Rte. 111** to continue the ride. Crossing Rte. 111, the rail bed starts behind the guardrail and enjoys quiet, wooded surroundings for the next 0.4 miles, crossing a new pedestrian bridge over the Pequonnock near the midpoint. Tree roots make the surface bumpy at some points and encroaching foliage narrows the width of the trail. It then emerges at a paved parking lot for a business, follows the pavement to **Spring Hill Rd.**, and resumes on the other side at an old dump site. The remaining third of a mile is overgrown and not recommended for biking.

DRIVING DIRECTIONS:

From Rte. 15, the Merritt Pkwy., take Exit 49 and follow Rte. 25 north. Take Exit 9 and follow Daniels Farm Rd. south for a half-mile toward Trumbull. At the end, turn right on Rte. 127 north and then immediately turn right on Tait Rd. Park on the side being careful not to block traffic.

To reach the Whitney Ave. parking lot, follow Rte. 127 north for 1.4 miles. Turn right on Rte. 111 north and continue for 1.6 miles, then turn right on Whitney Ave. Look for the parking lot 0.4 miles ahead on the right.

TOILET FACILITIES:

none on site

BIKE SHOPS:

Cycle Fitness, 630 Main St., Munroe, (203) 261-8683

Cycle Fitness, 3571 Main St., Stratford, (203) 377-8966

RAD Rob's All Star Bike Shop, 90 Bridgeport Ave., Shelton, (203) 924-2317

Spoke 'n Wheel, 2355 E. Main St., Bridgeport, (203) 384-8779

ADDITIONAL INFORMATION:

Pequonnock River Valley Park, c/o Sherwood Island State Park, P.O. Box 188, Green Farms, CT 06436, Tel. (203) 226-6983

2
Munroe Rail-Trail
Munroe

length: 3.7 miles
surface: hard-packed gravel
terrain: flat

Munroe's rail-trail quietly slips through town with easy biking on a broad, smooth surface and lots of leafy scenery. A short detour on roads disrupts the route near its midpoint.

BACKGROUND:

The trail follows the course of one of New England's first railroads, the former Housatonic Railroad which made its maiden run to Munroe in 1840. Operating passenger and freight service to Bridgeport, the line was acquired in the early 1890's by the New York, New Haven, and Hartford Railroad but began to struggle in the mid-1900's when automobile and truck transportation took hold. It was abandoned in 1962 and the rails and ties were immediately removed.

A group of local residents eventually urged the town to acquire the corridor for use as a trail and in the mid-1990's the town secured a federal grant for its development. The Munroe Rail-Trail opened in 1999 and its expansion has been proposed in two directions: northward to Botsford Station and southward to connect Trumbull's segment of the route, the Housatonic Rail Bed (Chapter 1).

The trail's location adjoining Wolfe Park, a town-owned recreation area, is an added benefit. The park's 300-plus acres offer swimming facilities, picnic areas, walking trails, and athletic fields. An admission fee is charged.

RULES OF THE TRAIL:

Posted rules for the use of the Munroe Rail-Trail are scarce but cyclists should use the accepted practices of riding at a safe speed, keeping to the right side, and signaling others before passing to avoid startling them. Do not block trail traffic when stopped. At several road intersections, cyclists should use care when crossing by coming to a complete stop, looking for oncoming cars, and assuming that drivers are unable to see you.

Trailhead signs state that horses and motorized vehicles are not allowed on the trail. Bicycles are prohibited from the trails that explore the Great Hollow Lake area at Wolfe Park.

ORIENTATION:

The Munroe Rail-Trail is aligned in the north-south direction and runs for 3.7 miles from the Newtown/Munroe border in the north to Wolfe Park in the south with a trailhead parking lot located near the midpoint at the intersection of Cutler's Farm Rd. and Pepper St. Most visitors use the southern half of the trail while the northern half has a more deserted feel.

Although it is not paved, the trail has a well-groomed appearance and affords safe, easy conditions for biking. The surface is 15 feet wide and has borders of mowed grass on each side and split-rail fencing placed for protection where steep bankings or other hazards exist. Road intersections have crosswalks painted on the pavement, metal posts to block vehicles from entering the trail, and stop signs to warn cyclists of the intersection. Mileage markers beside the trail plot the distance measured from Purdy Hill Rd. at the entrance to Wolfe Park.

TRAIL DESCRIPTION:

Starting at the trailhead parking lot at the intersection of **Cutler's Farm Rd.** and **Pepper St.**, follow the trail to the south (across Cutler's Farm Rd.) to reach Wolfe Park. The 1.3-mile trip begins with a gentle left-hand curve on a low, earthen causeway built through a swampy woodland. After three quarters of a mile, riders will notice that the scenery changes dramatically when the trail enters the **Wind Gap**, a 150-foot-deep pass between two hills lined with steep slopes, ledges, and boulders.

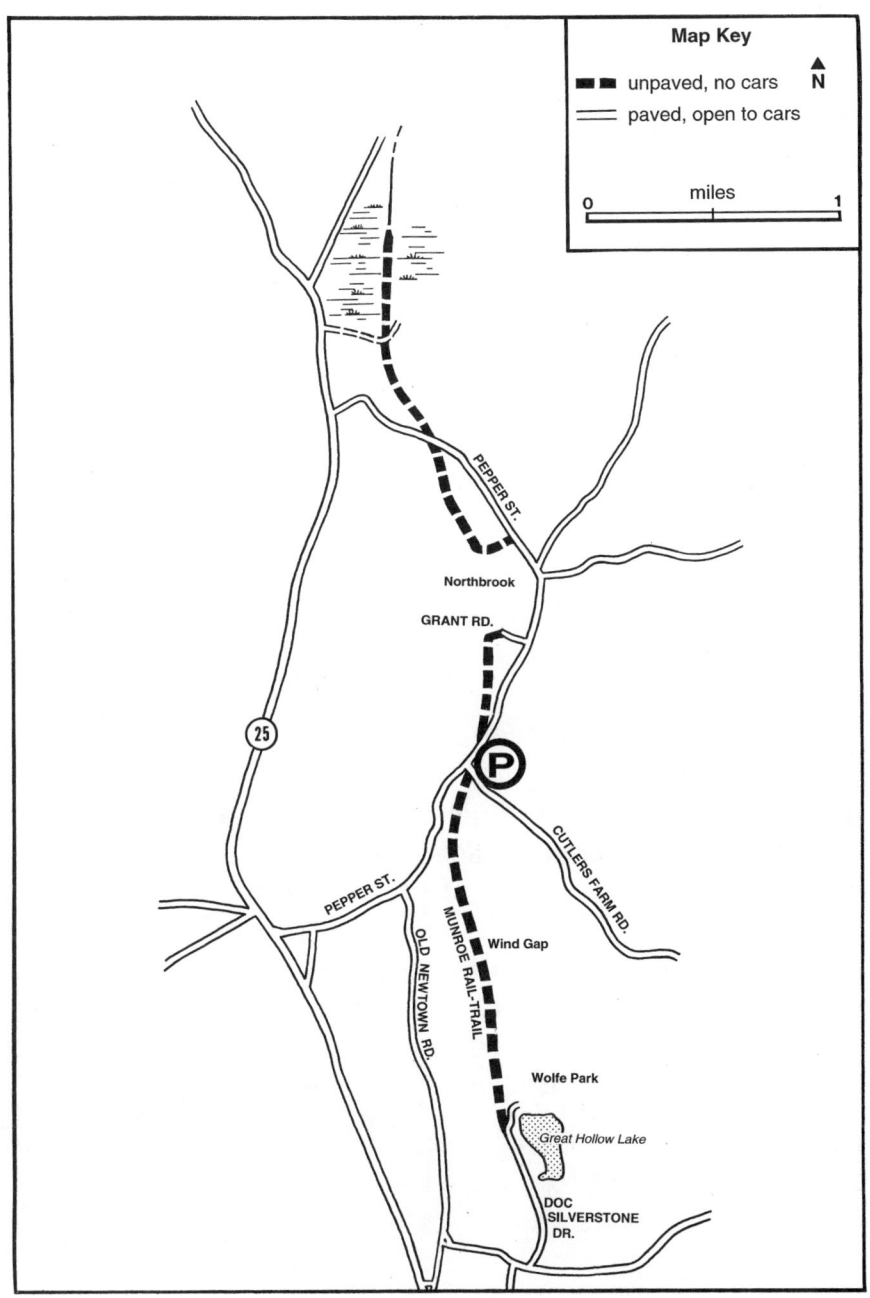

Map Key

- ■■■ unpaved, no cars
- —— paved, open to cars

N

miles
0   1

PEPPER ST.

Northbrook

GRANT RD.

25

PEPPER ST.

OLD NEWTOWN RD.

MUNROE RAIL-TRAIL

CUTLERS FARM RD.

Wind Gap

Wolfe Park

Great Hollow Lake

DOC
SILVERSTONE
DR.

Slicing through this opening, the trail hugs the right-hand slope as the passage widens into a small stream valley. The trail develops a slight downhill grade at this point which lasts for the remaining half-mile to **Doc. Silverstone Dr.**, an access road to **Wolfe Park**. Benches await beside the trail at this southern terminus with a fine view over the swimming beach at **Great Hollow Lake**. Bicyclists should note that the trails exploring Wolfe Park are reserved only for foot travel.

Turning north and heading in the opposite direction from the trailhead parking lot, the Munroe Rail-Trail extends for 2.4 miles to the border of Newtown. It crosses **Pepper St.** almost immediately and follows the edge of several fields for nearly a half-mile, then abruptly turns right on a 0.7-mile detour from the rail bed where the **Northbrook** residential development has blocked the original rail bed. Clearly marked by Bike Route signs, the detour begins on **Grant Rd.**, turns left on Pepper St. and continues for 0.4 miles, then turns left on a trail that rises on a small hill and returns to the rail line.

Continuing northward, the rail-trail runs for a half-mile to another intersection with Pepper St., crossing a stream and passing a few industrial sites along the way. Beyond Pepper St. the trail gets noticeably less use and weeds have encroached at the edges of the prepared surface. After slipping between a few ledge outcroppings, it crosses a private road and extends for the final third of a mile on a straight causeway built across a wetland to the town line. An overgrown footpath continues along the rail bed into Newtown from this endpoint.

DRIVING DIRECTIONS:

From Rte. 15, the Merritt Pkwy., take Exit 49 and follow Rte. 25 north. Where the divided highway ends, continue on Rte. 25 north for 3 miles to the village of Upper Stepney, turn right on Pepper St. and continue for 1 mile, then turn right on Cutler's Farm Rd. Turn immediately left on a one-way gravel road that is designated for rail-trail parking.

TOILET FACILITIES:

Toilets are available at Wolfe Park's Great Hollow Lake

BIKE SHOPS:

Bethel Cycle, 120 Greenwood Ave., Bethel, (203) 792-4640

Cycle Fitness, 630 Main St., Munroe, (203) 261-8683

RAD Rob's All Star Bike Shop, 90 Bridgeport Ave., Shelton, (203) 924-2317

World of Bikes, 317 S. Main St., Newtown, (203) 426-3335

ADDITIONAL INFORMATION:

Munroe Parks and Recreation Dept., Munroe Town Hall, 7 Fan Hill Rd., Munroe, CT 06468, Tel. (203) 452-5416

3
Larkin State Park Trail
Naugatuck - Southbury

length: 10.7 miles
surface: gravel
terrain: gentle slopes

A former railroad, the Larkin State Park Trail tames a forested terrain of hills and wetlands with an even passageway for bicycling, walking, and horseback riding. A few rough spots make wide bicycle tires preferable.

BACKGROUND:

The New York and New England Railroad completed this route between western Connecticut and New York in 1881 using the manual labor of Irish immigrants. Following the railroad's bankruptcy in 1894, the line became part of the New York, New Haven, and Hartford. Passenger service ended in 1931 during the Great Depression and freight service lasted until 1939, when the railroad ceased operations.

Charles L. Larkin saw the value of the abandoned rail bed as a linear park and in 1943 he gifted it to the state for use as a bridle trail. The wisdom of this vision is now evident not only on the trail which bears his name but on rail-trails throughout the state and the country.

RULES OF THE TRAIL:

Cyclists are asked to share the trail with others. Ride at a safe speed, keep to the right side, and give a friendly greeting before passing others to avoid startling them. Use extra caution when approaching horses, especially from behind, since they can be unfamiliar with bicycles and be prone to panic. Upon meeting a horse, bicyclists should make verbal contact with the rider well in advance so that the animal will feel safe and should wait for the horseback rider's advice before proceeding. Sometimes stopping at the side of the trail and dismounting your bike will be necessary.

The trail is open to passive uses from sunrise to sunset. Visitors are asked to avoid blocking trailhead gates when parking since work crews or emergency vehicles always need access.

ORIENTATION:

The trail is aligned in a mostly east-west direction with a designated parking lot located on Rte. 63 at the eastern terminus. Minimal parking spaces also exist at turnouts where the trail intersects Strongtown Rd. (Rte. 188), Christian St., and Towantic Hill Rd. south of Towantic Pond. Be careful not to block trailhead gates.

The highest elevation along the 10.7-mile route is at the midpoint between Towantic Hill Rd. and Christian St. with gentle slopes declining toward each endpoint. Most of the trail has a smooth, hard-packed surface but a few areas have exposed rocks, horse hoof prints, or brief detours at road crossings which hold rougher conditions. In general, conditions are smoothest at the eastern end and midsection of the trail and are roughest along parts of the western end.

Crosswalks do not exist at road intersections so use appropriate caution and assume that drivers do not see you. Although road intersections are numerous, much of the trail is remote so be prepared with water, snacks, and bike tools when attempting to ride the entire length.

TRAIL DESCRIPTION:

From the parking lot on **Rte. 63**, take the curving path uphill through the woods to the rail bed, reached in a short distance. Turn left and follow the firm, smooth surface westward, first as it slices through an outcropping of ledge and then as it passes a few housing developments on a slight uphill grade.

This incline lasts for about a mile with the exception of an abrupt drop to **Jones Rd.** at the site of a missing bridge. The trail travels high above the surrounding woods on two elevated grades which bridge low-lying areas, then

28

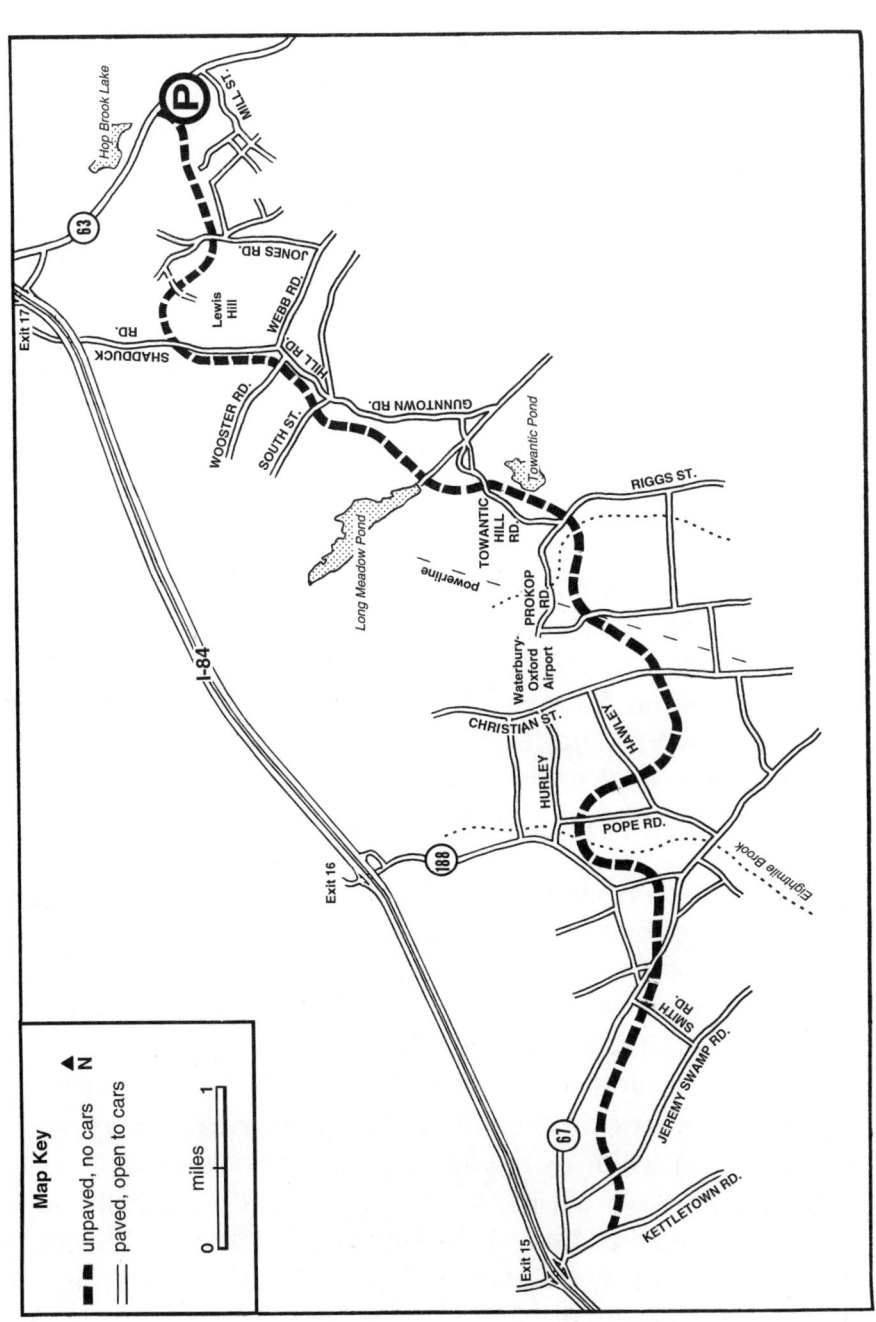

Map Key

N

■ ■ unpaved, no cars
━━ paved, open to cars

0   miles   1

hugs the slope of **Lewis Hill** and loops around its northern side where the incline begins to temporarily flatten.

Turning southward at the crossing of **Shadduck Rd.** after 2 miles, the trail cuts through more bedrock and tilts upward again on an incline which lasts for the next 2 miles. It crosses **South St.** at the site of another missing bridge, crosses two earthen causeways built across low spots in the terrain, and then passes the southern end of **Long Meadow Pond** which is barely visible behind a dam at a small settlement of houses. The rail bed has been filled at the intersection of **Towantic Hill Rd.** where a short path detours on the left side and scrambles up a banking to cross the pavement at the trail's 4.3-mile mark.

The next 1.9 miles are mostly flat and have a mowed border of grass for much of the way. The trail enters a more open environment near **Towantic Pond** and passes its boggy, western shoreline with a half-mile straightaway. After crossing a **powerline**, riders might notice low-flying aircraft approaching nearby **Waterbury-Oxford Airport**.

Christian St. marks the 6.2-mile point and the start of a slight downhill grade which lasts for the remaining 4.5 miles. The trail straightens as it crosses another causeway built across a wetland, then begins a northward turn to the right and leaves the rail bed for a short distance at the intersection of **Hawley Rd.** Returning to the rail bed, the trail reverses its course with a 180-degree turn back to the south, crossing **Pope Rd.** and a causeway over **Eightmile Brook** along the way.

The trail crosses **Rte. 188** (Strongtown Rd.) at the 8.3-mile mark and resumes its westerly course. The next half-mile deteriorates with a narrowing treadway from encroaching foliage, drainage problems where the trail passes through a cut in the hillside, and a rough detour at the intersection of busy **Rte. 67**. After crossing the road, follow the driveway downhill to the right and look for the rail bed to continue on the right side.

The downhill grade is more pronounced at this point

and suffers from more drainage problems for a short distance. The trail joins a driveway on the way to **Smith Rd.**, then crosses the pavement and takes a straight, smooth line for the next half-mile. Another detour is required at a missing bridge over **Jeremy Swamp Rd.** where a footpath drops down the embankment and climbs back to the rail bed on the other side. The last half-mile to **Kettletown Rd.** offers easy rolling over flat ground with a grassy surface.

DRIVING DIRECTIONS:

From I-84 westbound take Exit 17 and follow signs for Rte. 64 west. Turn left on Rte. 63 south and continue for 2.8 miles to the parking lot on the right.

From I-84 eastbound take Exit 17 and turn right on Rte. 63 south. Drive for 2.1 miles to the parking lot on the right.

From Rte. 8 take Exit 26 and follow Rte. 63 north for 2.5 miles to the parking lot on the left.

TOILET FACILITIES:

None provided

BIKE SHOPS:

Bike Rack, 1059 Huntingdon Ave., Waterbury, (203) 755-0347

Class Cycles, 105 Playhouse Corner, Southbury, (203) 264-4708

Road Rash Bicycles, 225 West St., Seymour, (203) 881-1834

ADDITIONAL INFORMATION:

Larkin State Park Trail, c/o Southford Falls State Park, Quaker Farms Rd., Southbury, CT 06488, Tel. (203) 264-5169

4
Middlebury Greenway
Middlebury

length: 4.8 miles
surface: pavement, stone dust
terrain: hilly, with some steep slopes

The Middlebury Greenway links the center and the outskirts of town with a healthy alternative for travel and recreation. From sunrise to sunset the path attracts walkers, runners, and cyclists eager to tackle its rolling hills while happily avoiding nearby traffic.

BACKGROUND:

The greenway follows the rail bed of a former trolley line which ran from the city of Waterbury to Middlebury and Woodbury. Opened in 1908 by the Connecticut Company, the trolley provided a major improvement for commerce and transportation in the area by allowing Middlebury's residents easy access to the city and Waterbury's population an enjoyable way to visit the countryside. In the warm season, the company offered open-air cars which brought crowds of visitors from Waterbury to Lake Quassapaug, a summer retreat in Middlebury. The ticket price was 15 cents.

The popularity of cars and buses forced the closing of the trolley line in 1930 and the tracks were quickly removed for scrap metal. After lingering for about 60 years, the route was reborn in 1992 as a multi-use trail stretching for 3.3 miles from Lake Quassapaug to Chase Rd. Additional construction in subsequent years has extended it eastward for another 1.5 miles to Rte. 63.

RULES OF THE TRAIL:

The trail is open to walkers, runners, and bicyclists. For safety reasons, in-line skating and skateboarding are not permitted. Cyclists are expected to yield to pedestrians and, when approaching from behind, should warn others before passing to avoid startling them. A sign at the trailhead reads, Take only photographs, leave only footprints, keep only memories.

ORIENTATION:

The greenway parallels Rte. 64 in roughly the east-west direction between Lake Quassapaug and Rte. 63. It is accessible from two parking lots, one at the high point of the trail near the western end and another at the intersection of Chase Rd. The western parking lot occupies the greenway's highest elevation so cyclists starting there should remember to save extra energy for their uphill return.

The 10-foot-wide trail has a paved surface for half the distance and a stone dust surface for the remainder, as displayed on the map. A few short portions of the greenway do not have a separated pathway and instead follow public roads.

An attractive landscape of plantings, grass borders, and benches adorns the trail, fencing protects it at steep bankings, and barricades prevent vehicles from entering at road intersections. Crosswalks guide trail users across most of the roads but several intersections have steep inclines and deserve caution, especially when riding with children.

TRAIL DESCRIPTION:

Starting at the western trailhead parking lot beside **Rte. 64** on the hill above **Lake Quassapaug**, the greenway heads in two directions. To the west, it lasts for only a third of a mile with a descent to a ballfield across from the Quassy Amusement Park, one of the area's most popular summer attractions. To the east, the trail runs for 4.5 miles with a mostly downhill trip to Rte. 63.

Riding eastward, bicyclists pass signs warning riders to use safe speeds on an impending downhill curve. The pavement tilts downward for a third of a mile on a moderate slope with a right-hand bend, crossing a few driveways near the bottom where riders must maneuver through barricade posts. Halfway down the hill on the opposite side of Rte. 64,

34

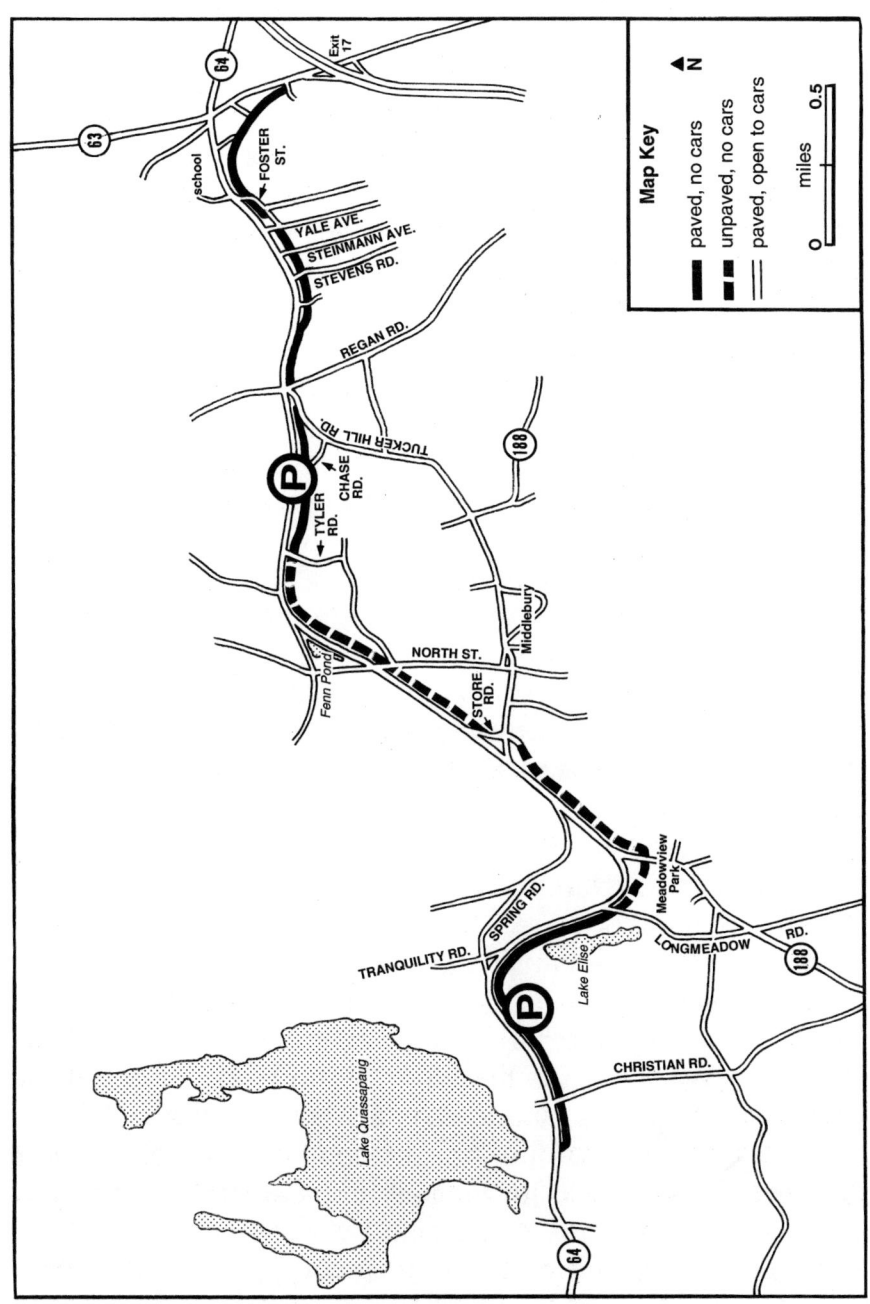

a small stone building which was once a trolley stop sits in the triangle formed at the intersection of **Tranquility Rd.** and **Spring Rd.**

The slope reverses to a slight incline at the bottom where a row of telephone poles is aligned in the middle of the path near **Lake Elise**. The trail crosses **Longmeadow Rd.** at the top of the rise, looses its pavement for a surface of crushed stone, and then curves back to the left on a slope above the playing fields of **Meadowview Park**. It then descends with a few curves to a small playground and parking lot and crosses **Rte. 188** about a mile from the main trailhead parking lot.

Here the surface changes to hard-packed stone dust and a 0.4-mile incline begins. The greenway follows Rte. 188 uphill to the merge of Rte. 64, then bends to the right alongside the roadway on a milder slope which is landscaped with shrubs, fencing, and a few benches. At the top, the trail veers from the edge of the road and descends on a rough gravel road along a powerline to a parking lot near the center of town.

Cross Rte. 188 on **Store Rd.** to continue the ride. (In the future, a proposed tunnel might carry the greenway underneath Rte. 188 at this point.) Follow the pavement of Store Rd. downhill for about a tenth of a mile and look for the greenway to resume on the right, just before Rte. 64.

The trail continues downhill on a gentle slope with a strip of trees and a banking providing extra separation from the roadway for a third of a mile until the intersection of North St., where the trail returns to the edge of the road. Reaching flat ground across from **Fenn Pond**, it crosses a wooden bridge over Goat Brook, bends to the right, and crosses **Tyler Rd.** at the start of another gradual descent. The next quarter-mile to the trailhead parking lot at **Chase Rd.** is screened from the traffic by another tree-covered banking and enjoys the natural scenery of the Goat Brook as it tumbles downhill.

Continuing eastward, the downhill run lasts for

another quarter-mile. The trail passes through a cut in a small hill where the original trolley line was blasted into bedrock, then reaches **Tucker Hill Rd.** at a low point near Hop Brook. The greenway follows the edge of Rte. 64 for the next quarter-mile up a short slope before separating from the roadway and descending across **Stevens Rd.** to Long Swamp Brook.

Here a cluster of road intersections deserves caution. Crossing **Steinmann Ave.**, the greenway climbs steeply to **Yale Ave.**, crosses the road and follows **Foster St.** for a short distance, then resumes with a separated pathway on the left. After crossing Foster St. again, the trail rounds a corner on a slope above Rte. 64 and then coasts downhill to the side of **Rte. 63** near Exit 17 of I-84.

DRIVING DIRECTIONS:

To reach the western trailhead parking lot near Lake Quassapaug take Exit 16 from I-84 and follow Rte. 188 north for 2.7 miles. Turn left on Rte. 64 west and continue for 1 mile to the parking lot on the left at the top of a hill. If you pass the Quassy Amusement Park, you have gone too far.

To reach the Chase Rd. trailhead parking lot, take Exit 17 from I-84 and follow signs for Rte. 64 west. From the intersection of Rte. 63, drive for 1.3 miles on Rte. 64 west and turn left on Chase Rd. Park in the lot immediately on the right.

TOILET FACILITIES:

Toilets are not provided at the trailhead, but they are available at the police station beside Meadowview Park.

BIKE SHOPS:

Bike Rack, 1059 Huntingdon Ave., Waterbury, (203) 755-0347
Class Cycles, 105 Playhouse Corner, Southbury, (203) 264-4708
Watertown Cycle Center, 1376 Main St., Watertown, (860) 274-9950

ADDITIONAL INFORMATION:

Middlebury Parks & Recreation Dept., 1212 Whittemore Rd., P.O. Box 392, Middlebury, CT 06762, Tel. (203) 758-2520

5
Salisbury Rail-Trail
Salisbury

length: 2.1 miles
surface: mowed grass, dirt
terrain: flat

Tucked in the hills of Connecticut's northwest corner, Salisbury's quiet rail-trail is a short but scenic route linking the town's two village centers with a smooth carpet of grass. Locals love the trail as a convenient connection for work and play.

BACKGROUND:

Salisbury, founded in 1741, was the source of some of the world's finest iron ore for nearly 200 years and earned the nickname Arsenal of the Revolution after it produced over 800 iron cannon during the Revolutionary War.

The town's railroad, originally called the Connecticut Western, was part of a line which was extended from Collinsville to Millerton, NY, in 1871 and linked Hartford with Poughkeepsie. Following the construction of a bridge over the Hudson River at Poughkeepsie in 1888, this railroad became one of the dominant lines between New England and New York.

Trucks and interstate highways eventually ended the railroad's business. The last train rolled down the tracks in 1965, the rails and ties were quickly removed, and the town later acquired this 2-mile section of the rail bed for use as a public trail.

RULES OF THE TRAIL:

Bicyclists are expected to yield to walkers, runners, and horseback riders. The trail is not heavily used but cyclists are asked to ride at a safe speed and alert others before passing them. Show proper respect for those who live nearby by keeping noise levels to a minimum and carrying out at least as much as you carry in.

ORIENTATION:

The trail is aligned in a mostly north-south direction paralleling Rte. 44 between the Salisbury village center and Lakeville. The trail exists in a relatively undeveloped state but the surface has mowed grass for most of the way, gates and barricades are in place at road crossings, and a few signs display information along the way.

No trailhead parking lot exists so visitors are advised to park on Library St. near the trail's northern terminus. Park beside the road being careful not to block traffic.

TRAIL DESCRIPTION:

Heading north from **Library St.**, the trail lasts for only about a half-mile. It begins by following the pavement of **Railroad St.** for less than a quarter-mile and then continues into the woods at a gate on the left side. Enclosed overhead by surrounding trees, the rail bed has a firm, earthen surface for easy rolling and passes the backyards of several homes before merging with a gravel driveway off **E. Main St. (Rte. 44**), where the public trail ends.

Heading south from Library St., the trail continues for 1.6 miles through mostly open surroundings of fields and wetlands. It starts with a bridge crossing of Wachocastinook Brook and follows the edge of a field which slopes downhill to the left with a pretty view. After a quarter-mile, the trail crosses **Salmon Kill Rd.**, turns slightly toward the southwest, and enters a scenic area of small ponds, brooks, and wetlands on a three-quarter-mile, straight-line course. Its green strip of grass is elevated above low-lying areas on each side with the exception of a shady cut through a hillside near the mid-point.

One mile south of Library St., the trail passes Salisbury's **sewage treatment plant** and follows its paved access road for a quarter-mile. Where the pavement turns hard right at the end of **Walton Rd.** the trail continues straight along the rail bed with a considerably narrower width of mowed grass and a thick cover of foliage along the

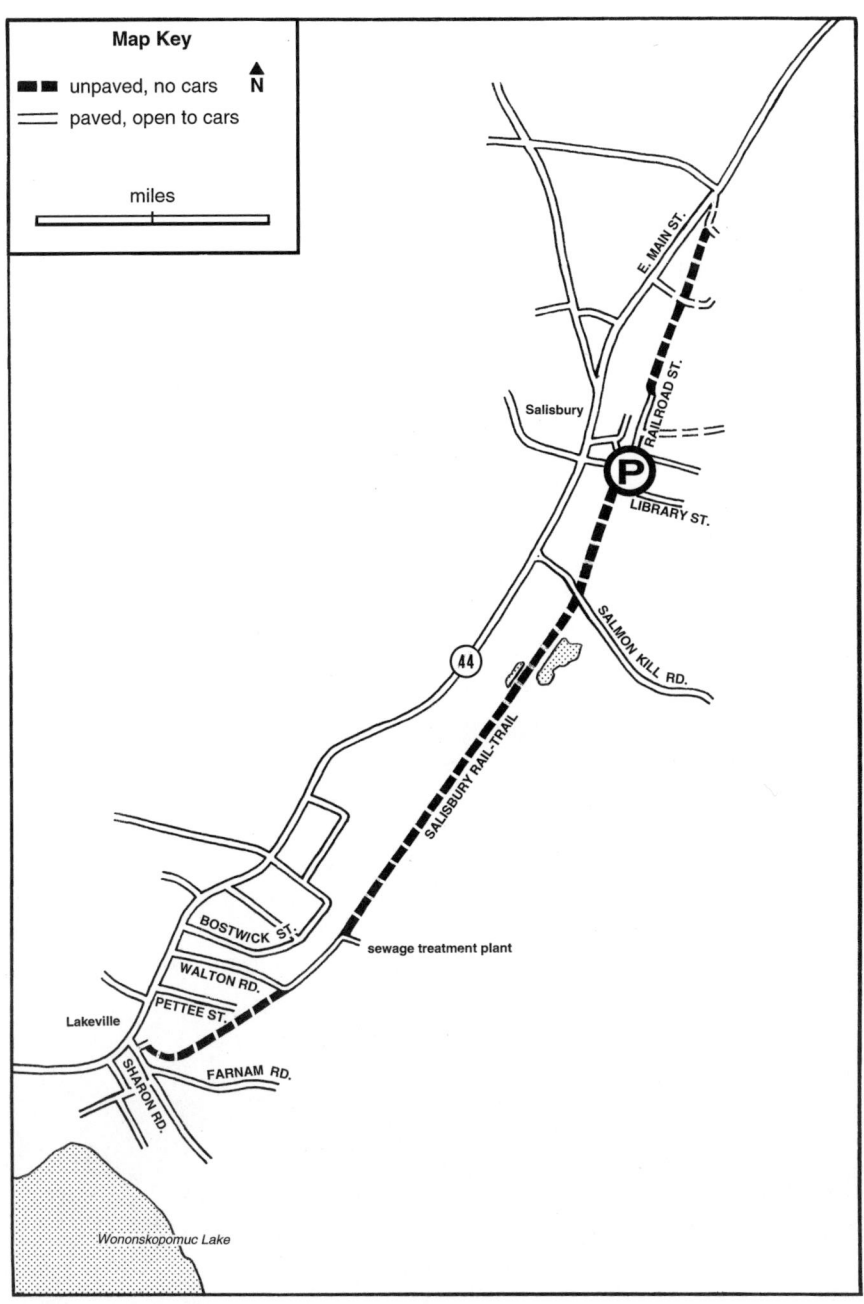

Map Key

■■ unpaved, no cars

═══ paved, open to cars

N

miles

E. MAIN ST.

RAILROAD ST.

Salisbury

P

LIBRARY ST.

SALMON KILL RD.

44

SALISBURY RAIL-TRAIL

sewage treatment plant

BOSTWICK ST.

WALTON RD.

PETTEE ST.

Lakeville

SHARON RD.

FARNAM RD.

Wononskopomuc Lake

sides. Although the surface remains reasonably smooth, the overgrowth blocks most views and gives a rougher look to the trail for the remaining quarter-mile to **Lakeville**.

The trail passes the end of **Pettee St.** and emerges on an elevated grade between a lumber yard and a ballfield. Before reaching the site of a missing iron bridge which spanned **Farnam Rd.** and Factory Brook, the trail veers to the right, descends the railroad grade beside a split rail fence, and skirts a ball field to reach **Sharon Rd.**

DRIVING DIRECTIONS:

Salisbury is located on Rte. 44 approximately 51 miles west of I-84 in Hartford and approximately 25 miles west of Rte. 8 in Winsted. Look for Library St. on the left in downtown Salisbury across from the town hall and beside the stone library. Continue on Library St. to the first hard right turn where the trail intersects on the right and Railroad St. intersects on the left. Park beside the road, being careful not to block traffic.

TOILET FACILITIES:

None are provided at the trail but they are available at the library when it is open.

6
Edgewood Park
New Haven

length: 1.2 miles
surface: paved
terrain: mostly flat with one hill

Edgewood Park has a short, beautiful piece of car-free pavement which is convenient to the city and well suited for in-line skating and biking with small children.

BACKGROUND:

Novelist Donald Grant Mitchell lived with his wife on this property from 1855 until his death in 1908. Farmland at the time, the estate was known as Edgewood and was loved for its small river, water views, and plentiful acreage. Mitchell appreciated the public's need for natural space and joined other landowners in donating acreage to the city in 1889, an act which inspired the acquisition of additional property by the city's newly formed Park Commission.

In subsequent years, the park has been developed in various stages with input from Frederick Law Olmsted in 1910 and Beatrix Farrand in 1937. Today's facilities include playgrounds, tennis courts, a skating rink, and playing fields.

RULES OF THE TRAIL

Bicyclists must remain on paved surfaces at Edgewood Park and are not allowed on unpaved trails. Given its proximity to population, the park is subject to heavy usage in fair weather so cyclists should ride responsibly and be courteous to others.

Visitors are requested to park only in designated locations and to help keep the park clean by not littering. Dogs must be leashed and owners must remove their pet's wastes. The park is open from sunrise to sunset.

ORIENTATION:

Surrounded by residential streets, Edgewood Park

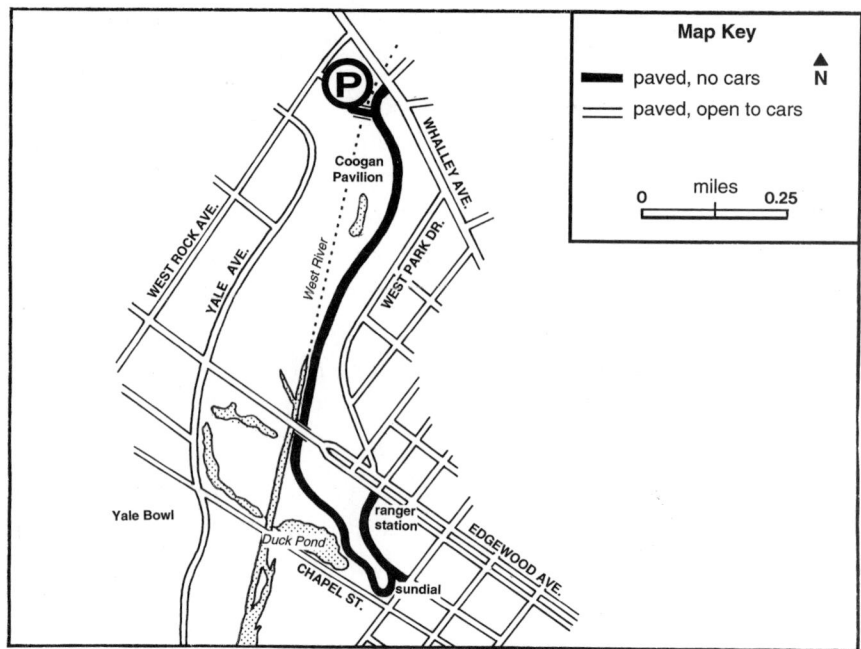

Map Key

▬ paved, no cars
═ paved, open to cars

▲ N

miles
0   0.25

forms a sliver of greenspace along the West River. The park's only paved route, an unnamed road, follows the acreage from the parking lot and tennis courts in the northwest to the ranger station and playground in the southeast.

TRAIL DESCRIPTION:

Starting at the parking lot off **West Rock Ave.** at the northern end of the park, look for a paved pathway leading into the woods from the left side of the tennis courts. It crosses the **West River** on a low, arched bridge and soon ends at the park's main road, which is unnamed.

Turn right and follow its broad surface past the **Coogan Pavilion**, where in-line skaters and skateboarders can find a half-pipe and an array of ramps in summer and ice skaters enjoy smooth ice in winter. The road runs southward from this point, first beside a strip of shaded lawns and then through a wooded area beside the West River. Near the midpoint it passes underneath **Edgewood**

Ave. at a multi-arch bridge beside the river, then bends left and emerges in the open area surrounding the **Duck Pond**. Benches and more lawns make this a popular place to relax.

The road winds uphill from the pond, climbing at a comfortable pace while approaching the edge of **Chapel St.**, then turns northward and reaches a T-intersection at the **sundial**. Turn left at this intersection to ride the last stretch of car-free pavement, a crescent-shaped road which returns to Edgewood Ave. and passes the **ranger station**, more lawns, and a playground.

DRIVING DIRECTIONS:

From I-95 take Exit 47 (or if southbound on I-91 take Exit 1) and follow Rte. 34 west for 1.9 miles to where it joins Rte. 10 heading north. Follow Rte. 10 north for 1.6 miles. Where Rte. 10 turns right on Fitch Ave., continue straight on Rte. 63 (Whalley Ave.) for a tenth of a mile, then turn left on West Rock Ave. Look for the parking lot on the left after a short distance.

From Rte. 15 (the Merritt Pkwy.), take Exit 59 and follow Rte. 69 south for a quarter-mile, then merge with Rte. 63 south. After 1.3 miles turn right on West Rock Ave. and look for the parking lot a short distance ahead on the left.

TOILET FACILITIES:

Toilets are located at the ranger station and at the Coogan Pavilion.

BIKE SHOPS:

Action Sports, 324 W. Main St., Branford, (203) 481-5511
Baybrook Bicycles, 243 Capt. Thomas Blvd., West Haven,
    (203) 933-4576
Baybrook Bicycles, 252 College St., New Haven, (203) 865-2724
Chapmans Orange Bicycle, 284 Boston Post Rd., Orange,
    (203) 795-5701
North Haven Bike, 476 Washington Ave., North Haven,
    (203) 239-7789
Rob's Bike Rack, 2348 Whitney Ave., Hamden, (203) 281-6660
Zane's Cycles, 105 N. Main St., Branford, (203) 488-3244

ADDITIONAL INFORMATION:

New Haven Dept. of Parks, Recreation, & Trees, 720 Edgewood Ave., New Haven, CT 06515, Tel. (203) 946-8021

7
East Shore Park
New Haven

length: 2 miles
surface: paved
terrain: flat

Located at the edge of New Haven Harbor, East Shore Park has a short but sweet network of paved trails with a flat, mile-long loop which is ideal for in-line skating or biking with kids.

BACKGROUND:

The park's history dates to 1923 when the property was deeded to the city. When New Haven Harbor was dredged in 1941, much of the excavated material was dumped at East Shore Park to fill its marshes and tidal pools and create the high, level ground that exists today.

Extensive improvements in the late 1970's and 1980's resulted in a landscape of lawns and planted trees as well as an array of recreational facilities which includes the paved bike paths. Other facilities at the park are baseball and soccer fields, tennis courts, an ice rink in winter, and playgrounds. In summer, swimmers head south past East Shore Park to the broad beach at Lighthouse Point Park.

RULES OF THE TRAIL:

East Shore Park's paved trails are popular with walkers and joggers so cyclists should plan on slow speeds. Keep to the right side of the trails and give a friendly warning before passing others to avoid startling them. Remember that pedestrians have the right of way.

ORIENTATION:

The park's trails curve and intersect frequently but the area's small scale and open landscape make it easy to find your way. The trails leave directly from the parking area and are bound by obvious landmarks that include the

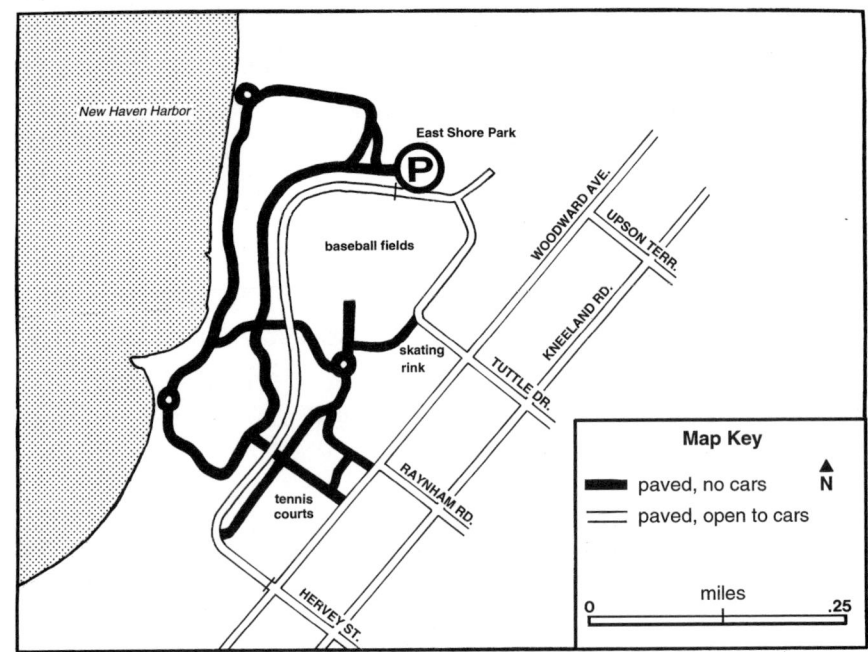

Map Key

■ paved, no cars
═ paved, open to cars

▲ N

miles

0 ——————— .25

athletic facilities to the east and the harbor to the west.

TRAIL DESCRIPTION:

Several trails explore the areas around the baseball fields and tennis courts but the most popular path for biking is the mile-long loop which leaves from the main parking area and ventures through the park's most scenic places. This route doubles as an exercise course and is equipped with a variety of workout stations along the way.

Following it in the clockwise direction, ride past the gate at the parking lot and continue straight on the trail that soon arcs gently toward the left, paralleling an access road beside two baseball fields. At 0.2 miles, keep straight at a four-way intersection where the trail enters a broader area of mowed lawns. The trail curves its way south for another 0.2 miles and then circles back to the right where it joins the harbor shoreline at a set of chin-up bars and returns to the north.

Soon after this turn, the path enters a circle of

50

pavement where a ring of benches invites a rest. It snakes through trees as it progresses northward from here and soon veers left at an intersecting trail that crosses the middle of the loop. A natural hedge of bushes shields most views of the water at first but the trail eventually gains a full exposure to the harbor's sights, and breezes, as it meanders at the edge of the park's lawns above the water.

Another circle of benches marks the 0.8-mile mark at a piece of high ground near the shoreline. Here the path turns inland and slips between a soccer field and the park's northern boundary beside a neighboring wastewater treatment plant. A final turn southward returns the path to the start of the loop at the parking lot.

DRIVING DIRECTIONS:
From I-95 northbound take Exit 50 and drive south on Woodward Ave. for 0.8 miles. Turn right at the park's entrance and continue to the large parking lot at the end of the drive.

From I-95 southbound take Exit 51 and follow Rte. 1 west for 0.9 miles. Turn left on Woodward Ave. and drive for 0.8 miles, then turn right at the park's entrance. Continue to the large parking lot at the end of the drive.

TOILET FACILITIES:
Toilets are available beside the ice skating rink.

BIKE SHOPS:
Action Sports, 324 W. Main St., Branford, (203) 481-5511
Baybrook Bicycles, 252 College St., New Haven, (203) 865-2724
Baybrook Bicycles, 243 Capt. Thomas Blvd., West Haven,
    (203) 933-4576
Chapmans Orange Bicycle, 284 Boston Post Rd., Orange,
    (203) 795-5701
North Haven Bike, 476 Washington Ave., North Haven,
    (203) 239-7789
Rob's Bike Rack, 2348 Whitney Ave., Hamden, (203) 281-6660
Zane's Cycles, 105 N. Main St., Branford, (203) 488-3244

ADDITIONAL INFORMATION:
New Haven Dept. of Parks, Recreation, & Trees, 720 Edgewood Ave., New Haven, CT 06515, Tel. (203) 946-8021

8
East Rock Park
Hamden

length: 2.3 miles
surface: paved, with accumulated leaves and twigs
terrain: hilly (not suitable for in-line skating)

East Rock Park's carriage roads curve gracefully through wooded slopes, cross stone arch bridges, and climb to a bird's eye view over New Haven. Each day they attract a healthy number of exercisers eager to enjoy the hilly terrain and natural scenery.

BACKGROUND:

Proposals to establish East Rock as a public park date from 1877 when Noah Porter, president of Yale College, sparked the creation of a commission to acquire and manage the land. Over the next fifty years, the commission was able to succeed in this effort with the help of donations of both land and money.

The park totals 425 acres and has a variety of features. Four carriage roads were created with donated funds in the park's early days and are now a highlight for visitors who can reach the summit by car or explore other areas that are closed to traffic. A 112-foot monument at the top is visible from miles away and was built in 1887 to honor soldiers who died in the Revolutionary War, the War of 1812, the Mexican War, and the Civil War. Athletic fields, 10 miles of hiking trails, picnic areas, and playgrounds are among the other attractions.

RULES OF THE TRAIL:

Bicycles are permitted on all paved roads but are prohibited from trails, which are intended for hiking. Trowbridge and English drives are closed to cars year-round while Hillhouse Dr. and the upper end of Farnam Dr. are closed to cars only Monday-Thursday (excluding holidays) from November 1 to March 31. Since the roads have slopes and sharp curves, bicyclists are cautioned to ride at safe speeds, keep to the right side, and be ready to encounter others.

Visitors are urged to help keep the park clean by putting garbage in the barrels provided. Dogs must be leashed at all times and owners are required to remove their pet's wastes. The park is closed from sunset to sunrise.

ORIENTATION:

East Rock Park's most dominant natural feature is its topography. The roads can disorient newcomers as they turn frequently in order to negotiate the terrain and will test the physical limits of some bicyclists where they face considerable slopes. The straightest, mildest option is Trowbridge Dr. while hillier, curvier conditions await on Farnam and English drives. Although parallel segments of the roads appear to be close together on the map, steep terrain separates them. No signs mark the roads.

DESCRIPTIONS:

From the parking lot at the northern end of the park, **Farnam Dr.** continues uphill toward the summit. The road is closed to car traffic from November 1 to March 31 on Mondays, Tuesdays, Wednesdays, and Thursdays (excluding holidays) and attracts light traffic during the remaining periods when it is open to cars. Speed limits are posted at 25 m.p.h.

Farnam Dr. leaves the open air of **North Meadow** and enters the shade of woods where mature rhododendron bushes adorn the roadside and various ground covers carpet the forest floor. After a third of a mile of gentle incline, Farnam Dr. forks right at the intersection of Trowbridge Dr. and then gets a bit steeper, curving through a switchback turn with an open view and then ending at the intersection of English Dr. at the 0.8-mile mark. Here **Hillhouse Dr.** continues the uphill tack for the remaining quarter-mile to the summit of **East Rock** (elev. 365') where cyclists can rest on the lawn beneath the war memorial and

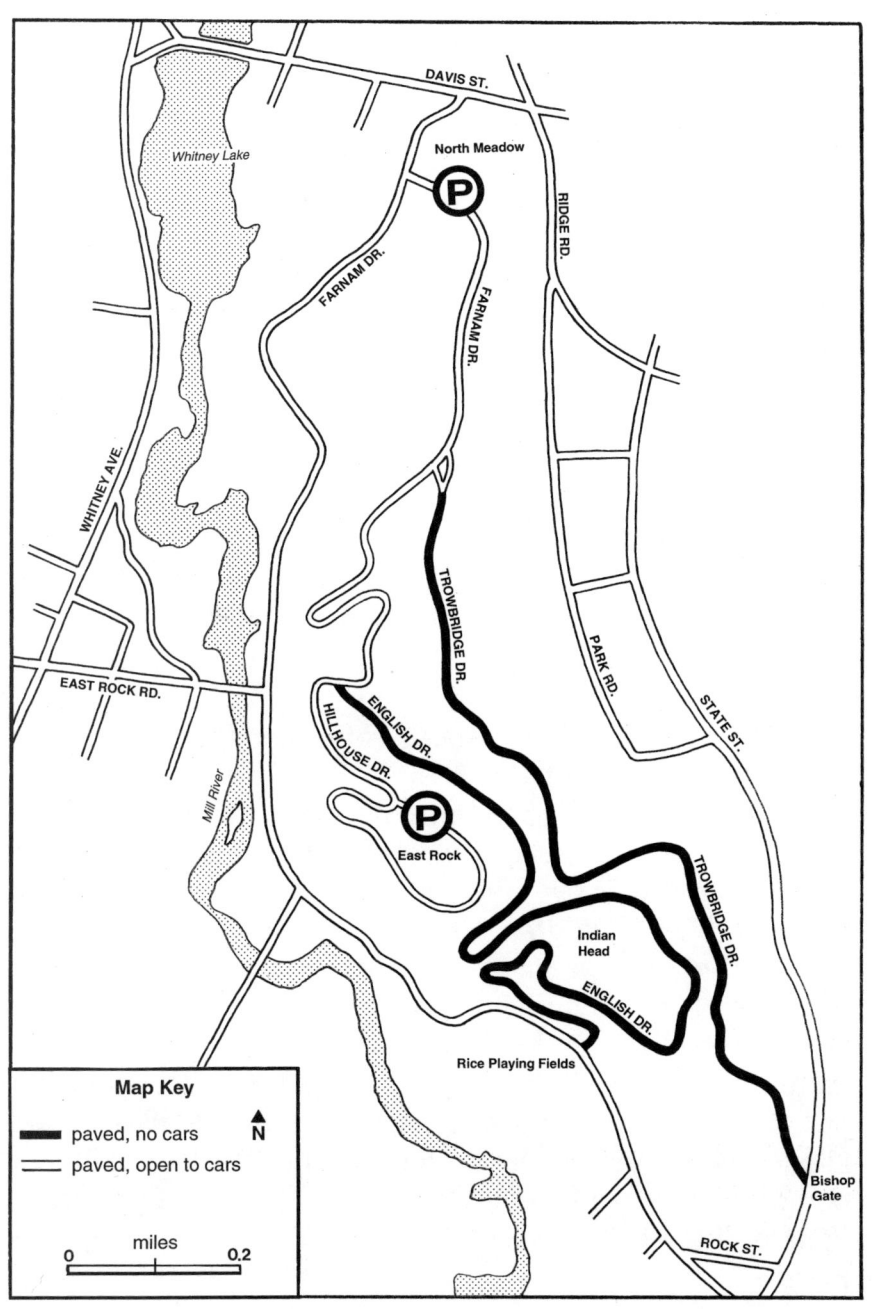

Map Key

▲
N

▬▬ paved, no cars

═ paved, open to cars

miles

0   0.2

gaze over the sight of New Haven and its harbor.

Mile-long **Trowbridge Dr.** begins on Farnam Dr. a third of a mile up from the parking lot and takes a gradual downhill route to **State St.** Closed to car traffic, it is perhaps the least used of the park's paved roads and accummulated leaves and twigs give its surface a forgotten look.

It starts with a taste of grandeur by crossing a stone arch bridge over a stream gulley, then continues along a flat course while turning frequently with the side of the slope. Here the road's flat profile and its smooth surface stand in marked contrast to the surrounding terrain which appears rocky and mountainous. More rhododendrons and mountain laurel bushes, planted during the park's early days, stand beside the road with sprawling, contorted limbs. A slight downhill grade develops after a half-mile and, after a right-hand corner, the road comes within sight and sound of State St. The remaining distance to **Bishop Gate** has a moderate downslope and a series of meandering curves.

English Dr. has steeper hills and sharper turns. Beginning at the intersection of Farnam and Hillhouse drives near the summit of East Rock, it descends for 1.3 miles to the base elevation at **Rock St.** After the first 0.4 miles of gradual descent, the road emerges from the forest shade at the bottom of an open cliff face below the summit, reverses direction at a hair-pin turn, and begins to circle the smaller hilltop known as **Indian Head**. English Dr. comes within sight of Trowbridge Dr. at a few points along this distance but a steep slope forms a barrier between the two routes. Halfway around Indian Head the road crosses a large stone arch bridge and then begins a final, half-mile descent which holds steeper pitches and several switchback corners. Limited visibility warrants slow speeds for cyclists along this portion of the road. Car-free pavement ends at a gate at the bottom of the hill on Rock St. across from the **Rice Playing Fields**.

DRIVING DIRECTIONS:

From I-91 take Exit 6. Turn left off the ramp on Willow St., then immediately left on State St. and continue for 1.4 miles to a traffic signal at Ridge Rd. Turn left on Ridge Rd. and continue for 0.4 miles, bear left on Davis St., then left at the park entrance. Take the first left to reach the parking lot on Farnam Dr.

From Rte. 15 (the Merritt Pkwy.) take Exit 61 and turn south on Whitney Ave. following signs to New Haven. Continue on Whitney Ave. for 2.8 miles and then turn left on Davis St. and drive for a half-mile. Turn right at the park entrance, then take the first left to reach the Farnam Dr. parking lot.

TOILET FACILITIES:

Toilet facilities are available during the warm season and are located at the Ranger Station on Orange St.

BIKE SHOPS:

Action Sports, 324 W. Main St., Branford, (203) 481-5511

Baybrook Bicycles, 252 College St., New Haven, (203) 865-2724

Baybrook Bicycles, 243 Capt. Thomas Blvd., West Haven,
   (203) 933-4576

Chapmans Orange Bicycle, 284 Boston Post Rd., Orange,
   (203) 795-5701

North Haven Bike, 476 Washington Ave., North Haven,
   (203) 239-7789

Rob's Bike Rack, 2348 Whitney Ave., Hamden, (203) 281-6660

Zane's Cycles, 105 N. Main St., Branford, (203) 488-3244

ADDITIONAL INFORMATION:

New Haven Dept. of Parks, Recreation, & Trees, 720 Edgewood Ave., New Haven, CT 06515, Tel. (203) 946-8021

   East Rock Ranger Station: (203) 946-6086

   Park Security Office: (203) 946-7268

9
West Rock Ridge State Park
Hamden, New Haven

length: 8.5 miles
surface: paved (except for Lake Wintergreen loop)
terrain: hilly (not suitable for in-line skating)

West Rock Ridge's paved hilltop roads require a sizeable uphill effort but reward pedalers with great views over the New Haven area. Nearby, an unpaved loop circles a small lake with gentler slopes.

BACKGROUND:

The first settlers found the terrain around West Rock Ridge to be too rough for farming but made good use of its timber, firewood, and stone. As the surrounding population grew and open space dwindled, West Rock became a popular place for residents to enjoy the outdoors and by the late 1800's visitors were ascending a new carriage road to the top of the hill and marveling at the distant views.

The state formed this 1500-acre park in 1977 by uniting parcels of land previously owned by the city of New Haven, the South Central Regional Water Authority, and others.

RULES OF THE TRAIL:

West Rock Ridge State Park attracts many activities, and bicyclists are expected to be considerate of others and to yield when necessary. Ride at a safe speed and alert others of your approach to avoid startling them.

Bicyclists should not be fooled by the abandoned appearance of the northern segment of Baldwin Dr. Work vehicles occasionally use the route to reach communication towers and other sites at the top of the ridge and other bicyclists, walkers, and runners make use of the road in all seasons of the year. Especially when descending through the steep, hairpin corners, cyclists should ride at a safe speed, keep to the right and be ready to encounter others on the road.

The park is open from 8:00 AM to sunset. Dogs must be leashed.

ORIENTATION:

Aside from the mountain biking trails, three options exist for bicycling at the park. The northern leg of Baldwin Dr. offers a 5.6-mile, car-free stretch of pavement that ascends the steep slope and then follows the flat, forested crest of the ridgeline with viewpoints at intervals along the way.

The southern leg of Baldwin Dr. is open to cars on weekends during the warm season and climbs for 1.2 miles to a panoramic view of New Haven at South Overlook. Both routes are accessed from the Nature Center parking lot across Wintergreen Ave.

A third option circles Lake Wintergreen in the park's lower elevations with milder terrain and a 1.6-mile, unpaved surface which starts from the trailhead on Main St.

TRAIL DESCRIPTIONS:

Starting at the Nature Center parking lot, turn left on Wintergreen Ave. and look for the entrance to **Baldwin Dr.** on the right after a short distance. The road is named after Simeon Baldwin, governor of Connecticut from 1911 to 1915, who bequeathed funds for its construction in 1927. Ride past the gate and turn right where the road forks at the base of the hill.

Heading north, this 5.6-mile stretch of road climbs to the top of the ridgeline, follows it to the park's northern reach, and then descends to the end of West Shepard St. The road begins to climb immediately with a strenuous, 0.8-mile incline which provides brief respites at 3 hairpin corners. The paved surface, cracking with age and narrowing from encroaching foliage, leads bicyclists smoothly upward past the entrance to the **Wilbur Cross Pkwy.** tunnel to the first hairpin corner, reached in less than a quarter-mile. The road gains the top of the ridge a short

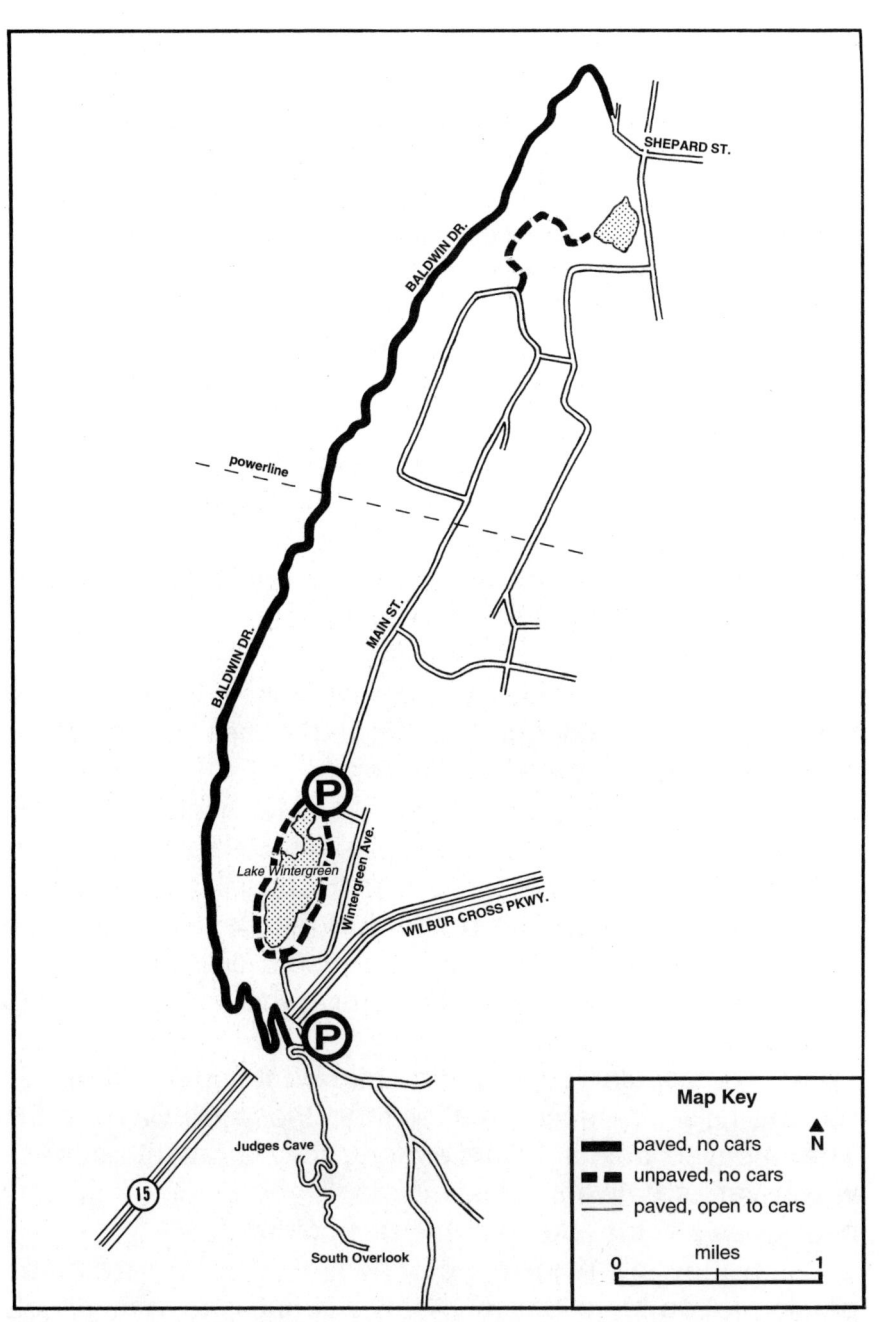

SHEPARD ST.

BALDWIN DR.

powerline

BALDWIN DR.

MAIN ST.

P

Lake Wintergreen

Wintergreen Ave.

WILBUR CROSS PKWY.

P

Judges Cave

15

South Overlook

Map Key

N

▬▬▬ paved, no cars

▬ ▬ unpaved, no cars

═══ paved, open to cars

miles

0   1

distance beyond the third switchback and offers a western view before turning a final time back to the north.

Baldwin Dr. straightens at this point on a relatively flat, 0.6-mile segment which is shaded by hardwood forest. Note that a few footpaths diverge on the left (west) side of the road to reach the top of an open cliff face where extreme caution should be used. A downward slope follows this straightaway and allows cyclists to coast for a quarter-mile before the road tilts uphill on an incline which lasts for about a half-mile.

Another mile of relatively flat and straight riding ensues before the road rises on a short uphill, crosses beneath a set of **powerlines**, and begins a rolling, up-and-down course for the remaining 2.5 miles. Turnouts in the pavement mark several viewpoints along the way. At the end, the road drops on one of its steepest slopes, turns to the south at a barricade blocking vehicle entry, and descends to the end of **West Shepard St.**

The southern leg of Baldwin Dr. is shorter, more heavily visited, and open to cars on weekends during the warm season. Forking left at the bottom near the entrance gate, the road climbs at an easier pace for 0.7 miles to a second fork. Turning left, riders ascend for another half-mile to **South Overlook** where an unobstructed view spreads southward over New Haven and Long Island Sound. Turning right, riders soon reach **Judges Cave**, a formation of boulders where in 1661 two members of Parliament hid from officers of the Crown after signing the death warrant of King Charles I.

The popular loop around **Lake Wintergreen** is not flat but the hills are much smaller than those on Baldwin Dr. The unpaved trail is 1.6 miles long, has a smooth surface which varies between crushed stone and packed dirt, and offers views of the lake at numerous points.

Following it in the clockwise direction from the parking lot on **Main St.**, face downhill and turn immediately left on the trail that extends southward in a straight line for a quarter-mile. It rises over a knoll, forks left at a dam containing the lake, and descends below the dam and into the woods. Passing a service building beside **Wintergreen Ave.** at the south end of the lake, the trail scrambles up its steepest hill and proceeds straight through a four-way intersection on its return to the north. The last leg measures three quarters of a mile and features gently rolling terrain with glimpses of the lake through the trees. Turn right at the next four-way intersection, cross a bridge over Wintergreen Brook, and climb the hill to return to the trailhead parking lot.

DRIVING DIRECTIONS:

From Rte. 15 (Wilbur Cross Pkwy.), take Exit 60 and follow Rte. 10 south, then turn right on Benham St. and drive for 2 miles to the end. Turn left on Main St. and look for the Lake Wintergreen trailhead parking lot 0.5 miles ahead on the right at a sharp, left-hand turn.

To reach the Baldwin Dr. trailhead, continue on Main St. for a short distance to the end, turn right on Wintergreen Ave., and look for the Nature Center parking lot on the left after the road passes underneath the Wilbur Cross Pkwy. The entrance to Baldwin Dr. is a short distance ahead on the right.

TOILET FACILITIES:

Toilets are not provided.

BIKE SHOPS:

Baybrook Bicycles, 252 College St., New Haven, (203) 865-2724
Baybrook Bicycles, 243 Capt. Thomas Blvd., West Haven,
   (203) 933-4576
North Haven Bike, 476 Washington Ave., North Haven,
   (203) 239-7789
Rob's Bike Rack, 2348 Whitney Ave., Hamden, (203) 281-6660

ADDITIONAL INFORMATION:

West Rock Ridge State Park, c/o Sleeping Giant State Park, 200 Mount Carmel Ave., Hamden, CT 06518, Tel. (203) 789-7498

Connecticut Dept. of Environmental Protection, 79 Elm St., Hartford, CT 06106-5127, Tel. (860) 424-3200
web: http://dep.state.ct.us

10
Farmington Canal Greenway
Cheshire - Hamden

length: 8.3 miles
surface: paved, with gravel walking trail on one side
terrain: gentle slopes

One of Connecticut's most popular bike paths, the Farmington Canal Greenway hosts a colorful parade of in-line skaters, runners, walkers, and cyclists throughout the year. The shady rail-trail follows the route of a historic canal for much of its length and visits two interesting town-owned parks along the way.

BACKGROUND:

The Farmington Canal was completed between New Haven and Farmington in 1828 and extended to Northampton, Massachusetts in 1836 to facilitate commerce between the seaport and the interior countryside. Measuring over 80 miles in length, it was the longest canal ever built in New England and one of the most complex requiring 28 locks to meet changes in elevation, 13 culverts to allow streams to flow beneath the canal, 3 aqueducts to carry the canal over rivers, and 135 bridges for local roads. The canal struggled to generate adequate revenues to repay these costs and closed in 1848 when a railroad began operation along the same route.

The railroad lasted until 1982 when a flood destroyed a section of the line in Cheshire. A short time later, the Farmington Rail to Trail Association was established to convert the route to a bike path and by the mid-1990's the towns of Hamden and Cheshire had acquired the property and had begun designing and constructing the trail. Proposed extensions include New Haven in the south and Southington in the north. The trail will be a main artery in Connecticut's growing network of bike paths and is one of the first established segments of the proposed East Coast Greenway, a route linking Maine to Florida.

Rules are posted at the main points of entry. Cyclists are asked to travel at a safe speed, keep to the right side, yield to pedestrians, and give an audible warning when passing. Stop at all road intersections and look for cars, remembering that drivers might not be able to see you. When stopping to rest, step off the trail to allow others to pass unimpeded. Note that the gravel paths running beside the paved trail are reserved for foot traffic.

Dogs must be leashed and their wastes removed. Trash recepticles are not present so plan to carry out what you carry in. The trail is open from dawn to dusk.

ORIENTATION:

The trail is marked as the Farmington Canal Greenway in Hamden and as the Farmington Canal Linear Park in Cheshire. It is aligned in the north-south direction and crossed by roads at regular intervals where crosswalks alert motorists, stop signs warn trail users, and metal posts block vehicles from entering the trail. Street names are posted at intersections along the Hamden section of the trail to inform trail users of their location.

The paved surface is 10-12 feet wide with borders of mowed grass on each side. The trail's profile is generally flat but it tilts to the south with a slight pitch on most sections. Exceptions to this are two detours along the Hamden portion of the rail line, one opposite Mt. Carmel Ave. and the other beside Sherman Ave., where the trail encounters steeper slopes.

Trailhead parking exists at five locations along the trail as noted on the map. One of the most popular starting points is Lock 12 Park in Cheshire where toilets, a drinking fountain, picnic area, and telephone are provided.

TRAIL DESCRIPTION:

Starting at **Lock 12 Park** on **North Brooksvale Rd. (Rte. 42)** in Cheshire, the trail extends in two directions.

66

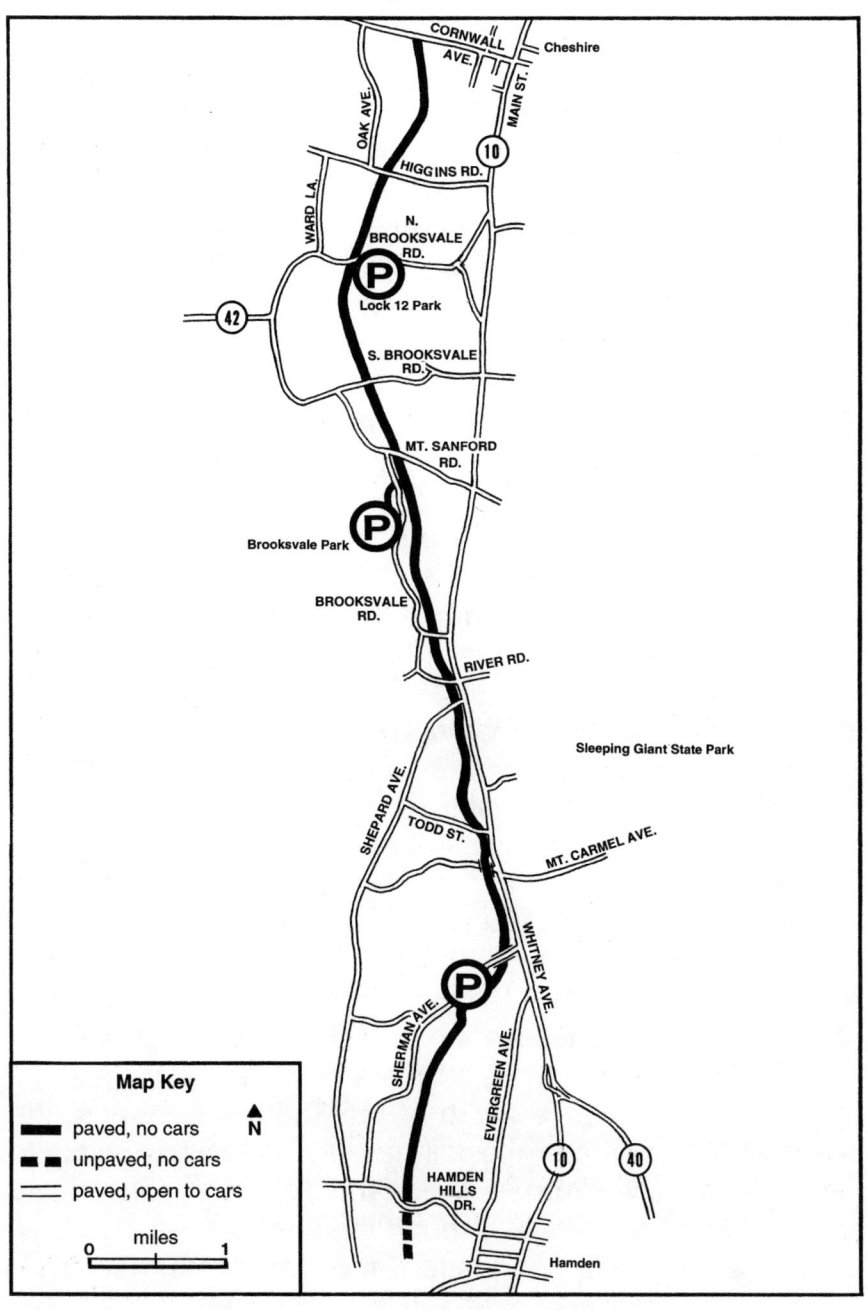

Heading north (turning right on the bike path when coming from the parking lot), it runs for 1.6 miles to the terminus at **Cornwall Ave.** with flat, straight, and shady conditions. It crosses **Higgins Rd.** near the midpoint and follows the canal bed for most of the way.

Heading south (turning left on the bike path when coming from the parking lot), 6.7 miles of car-free pavement extend through the neighboring town of Hamden. The bike path leaves North Brooksvale Rd. and passes **Lock 12 Park**'s restored lock, lock keeper's house, and museum on the left within a third of a mile. Rest rooms and a drinking fountain are also located here.

Continuing southward, the trail leaves the park on a stone arch bridge over the canal and follows the side of the channel through the shade of woods. It emerges in a semi-open area before crossing **South Brooksvale Rd.** 0.9 miles from North Brooksvale Rd., then follows split-rail fencing for the next half-mile to **Mt. Sanford Rd.** at the Hamden line.

The bike path follows a dry portion of the canal bed for another third of a mile to a sign and intersecting trail on the right which leads to Hamden's **Brooksvale Park** where a display of farm animals, a small playground, and several playing fields form a popular recreation area. A trailhead parking lot also makes this a potential starting point.

Continuing, the bike path follows the remnants of the canal, crosses a set of powerlines, and hits **Brooksvale Rd.** about 2.6 miles from the Lock 12 parking lot. It meets **River Rd.** and **Shepard Ave.** within the next half-mile, passes behind several businesses, and reaches another parking lot at **Todd St.** about 4.1 miles from the Lock 12 parking lot.

A short distance south of the Todd St. crossing, the bike path detours from the rail bed and descends gently to the edge of busy **Whitney Ave.** (**Rte. 10**) where fences and crosswalks guide the trail through the tight spaces of a retail area. Leaving this congestion, the trail contends with a sizeable uphill slope as it returns to the rail bed.

Next, it slips beneath a bridge carrying **Sherman**

Ave. and then veers off the rail bed and rises on the slope of a second detour at another trailhead parking lot. The bike path follows a guardrail beside Sherman Ave. for a quarter-mile then arcs left, returns to the rail line, and runs for another 1.4 miles with long, flat straightaways in wooded surroundings. The pavement ends below a bridge carrying **Hamden Hills Dr.** but a dirt trail continues southward.

DRIVING DIRECTIONS:
To reach Lock 12 Park in Cheshire from I-91, take Exit 10 and follow Rte. 40 north for 2.5 miles to the end. Turn right on Rte. 10 north and continue for 5.9 miles, then turn left on Rte. 42 west. The park is a mile ahead on the left.

To reach Lock 12 Park from I-691, take Exit 3 and follow Rte. 10 south to Cheshire. Turn right on Rte. 42 west and continue for one mile to the park on the right.

To reach the Sherman Ave. trailhead in Hamden from I-91, take Exit 10 and follow Rte. 40 north for 0.9 miles to the end, then turn left on Sherman Ave. Parking is ahead on the left.

To reach Brooksvale Park in Hamden from I-91, take Exit 10 and follow Rte. 40 north for 2.5 miles to the end. Turn north on Rte. 10 and continue for 3 miles, then turn left on Brooksvale Ave. The parking lot is 0.7 miles ahead on the left.

TOILET FACILITIES:
Find toilets at Lock 12 Park in Cheshire.

BIKE SHOPS:
Baybrook Bicycles, 252 College St., New Haven, (203) 865-2724
Cheshire Cycling, 209 W. Main St., Cheshire, (203) 250-9996
Rob's Bike Rack, 2348 Whitney Ave., Hamden, (203) 281-6660
Wallingford Bike, 218 N. Colony Rd., Wallingford, (203) 265-2998

ADDITIONAL INFORMATION:
Farmington Canal Rail-Trail Association, 940 Whitney Ave., Hamden, CT 06517

Parks and Recreation Dept., 559 S. Main St., Cheshire, CT 06410, Tel. (203) 272-2743

Parks and Recreation Dept., Hamden, CT 06518, Tel. (203) 287-2579

11
Farmington Valley Greenway
Farmington - Suffield

length: 4 sections totaling 15.6 miles
surface: pavement
terrain: gentle slopes

When completed, the Farmington Valley Greenway stands to be Connecticut's grandest rail-trail, a 25-mile passageway linking five towns with car-free commuting and recreation.

BACKGROUND:

The greenway follows the route of a former canal which was completed between New Haven and Farmington in 1828 and extended to Northampton, MA in 1836 to facilitate commerce between the seaport and the interior countryside. Measuring over 80 miles in length, it was the longest canal ever built in New England and one of the most complex requiring 28 locks to meet changes in elevation, 13 culverts to allow streams to flow beneath the canal, 3 aqueducts to carry the canal over rivers, and 135 bridges for local roads. The canal struggled to generate adequate revenues to repay these costs and closed in 1848 when a railroad began operation along the same route.

When the railroad ceased using the tracks in 1988, local citizens formed the Farmington Valley Trails Council to promote its conversion to a recreational trail. Construction started in 1994 after federal funding was secured and after additional support was approved by each of the five area towns, and it has progressed in phases in subsequent years. Proposed extensions would carry the trail south to connect both the Farmington River Trail in Farmington (Chapter 12) and the Farmington Canal Greenway in Cheshire (Chapter 10) and a northerly extension could eventually reach Northampton, MA.

TRAIL POLICIES:

Trail users should travel on the right side and pass on the left. When approaching others from behind, give an audible signal to avoid startling them. The trail can be busy with walkers, runners, in-line skaters, and other cyclists so ride at an appropriate speed and stay alert. Be especially careful in the presence of children since their movements can be unpredictable. At road intersections, stop and look both ways before entering the roadway and assume that drivers do not see you.

Keep dogs leashed, remove their wastes, and help keep the trail litter-free by carrying out at least as much as you carry in. The area is open from sunrise to sunset. Since each town has its own set of policies for use of the trail, watch for trailhead signs for additional regulations.

ORIENTATION:

The greenway will run from Farmington in the south to the Massachusetts border in Suffield in the north when it is completed. It currently exists in 4 sections: 8.7 miles from Rte. 4 in Farmington to Rte. 10 near Stratton Brook Rd. in Simsbury; 3.5 miles from Drake Hill Rd. in Simsbury to the East Granby town line; 2.5 miles in East Granby from Rte. 189 to Copper Hill Rd.; and 0.9 miles in Suffield near Phelps Rd. The Farmington-to-Simsbury stretch has a hilly, 1.8-mile detour from the rail-bed which is partly on roads.

The paved surface measures 10 feet wide with grass borders and protective fencing where necessary. Stop signs alert trail users at road crossings, crosswalks warn motorists, and barricades prevent vehicles from entering the trail. Parking lots provide access to each section.

TRAIL DESCRIPTION:

Starting at the **Brickyard Rd.** trailhead in Farmington, turn left to reach the greenway's current southern terminus after 0.8 miles of riding. Trees screen the trail from neighboring homes and businesses and split-rail fencing lines steep bankings along the way. The developed trail ends at a wooden barricade above Rte. 4 but future bridge reconstruction will allow it to reach Red Oak Hill Rd. near the end of the Farmington River Trail (Chapter 12).

Heading north from Brickyard Rd., the trail enters Avon along a straightaway with a faint downhill to the crossing of Chidsey Brook. After crossing **Thompson Rd.** after 1.5 miles, it enters a tunnel of foliage from nearby trees for the next half-mile until open sky returns after **Scoville Rd.** Here the trail straightens beside a row of telephone poles for a mile to **Country Club Rd.**, enjoying a slight downhill grade for most of the way.

The greenway leaves the rail bed as it approaches **Avon** center 3.7 miles north of the Brickyard Rd. trailhead and begins a 1.8-mile detour on a combination of local roads and separated pathway. Green, Bike Route signs mark the way. Turning left at the end of the paved rail bed, the route immediately emerges at the Avon DPW and follows its driveway northward to **Arch St.**, crosses the road and follows **Security Dr.** up a long hill to the end, then turns right on **Darling Dr.** Look for a separated pathway on the left before **W. Main St. (Rte. 44)** at the bottom of the slope.

It drops to a tunnel underneath W. Main St. and emerges at the police station parking lot. Following the Bike Route signs, turn right on Climax Heights Rd., turn left on the separated bike path beside **Ensign Dr.**, then turn right at **Fisher Dr.** and cross **Rte. 10** at the traffic signal. The trail resumes at a trailhead parking lot on the other side and returns to the rail bed in a tenth of a mile where the detour ends. A short spur runs along the rail bed to the right (south) for 0.2 miles while the greenway heads to the left.

Continuing northward, it passes signs for the **Nod Brook Wildlife Management Area** which preserves green space along the **Farmington River** on the right side. The trail then enters Simsbury and hits a number of road intersections, the busiest being another crossing of Rte. 10 about 1.1 miles north of the Avon detour. Since traffic can be heavy and many motorists do not see the bike path, use extra caution when crossing. On the other side, the

▲ continued at bottom of next page ▲

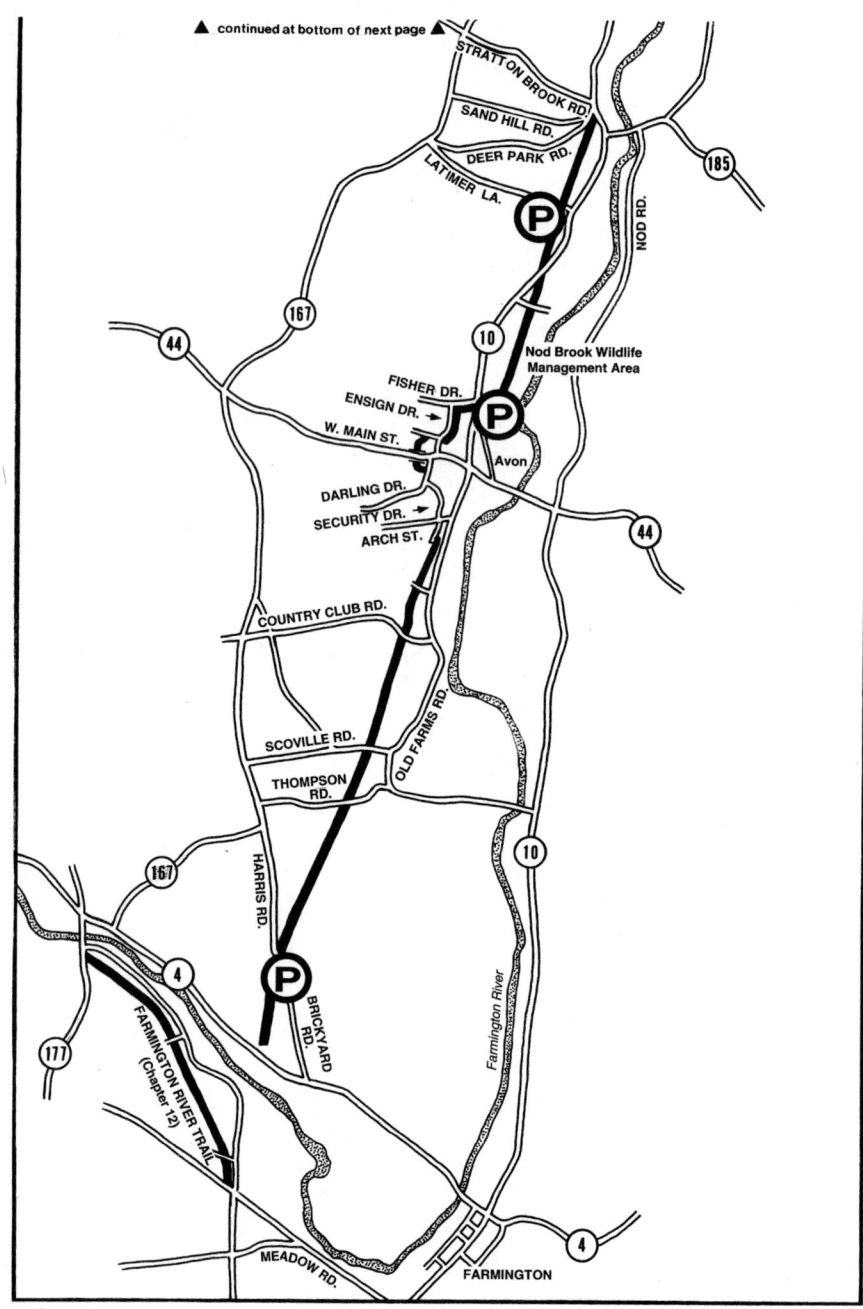

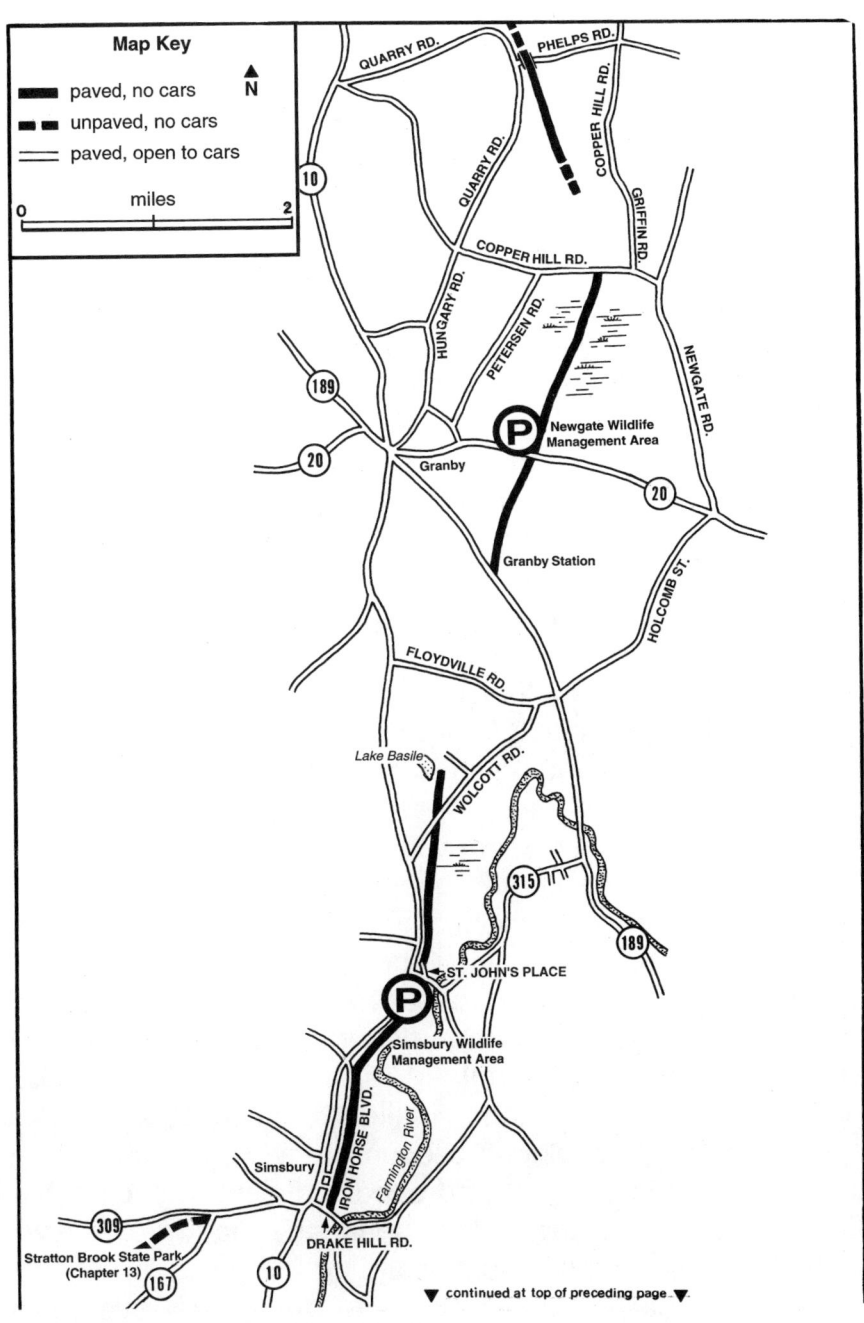

▼ continued at top of preceding page ▼.

greenway runs for another 1.3 miles along an open corridor of telephone poles, crossing **Latimer La.** at a trailhead parking lot and dipping at a few low points where wooden fencing corrals the trail through wetlands. This section of trail ends where it reaches Rte. 10 near **Stratton Brook Rd.**

The greenway resumes 1.8 miles to the north on **Drake Hill Rd.** at the center of **Simsbury.** It parallels a wooden guard rail beside **Iron Horse Blvd.** for the first mile passing between the downtown shopping area and a conservation area. Before reaching Rte. 10, the trail forks right and enters the green surroundings of the **Simsbury Wildlife Management Area** where an overlook allows a view over the Farmington River. A wide swathe of grass borders the trail along this stretch. It then merges at the foot of an embankment below Rte. 10 and crosses **Rte. 315** near a trailhead parking lot 2 miles north of Drake Hill Rd.

After a short gap the greenway continues from nearby **St. John's Place.** Passing a commercial area, it tilts downhill to a wetland, rises to the intersection of **Wolcott Rd.**, and runs for another 0.3 miles to **Lake Basile** at the East Granby town line, 3.5 miles from Drake Hill Rd.

A 2.6-mile detour on **Wolcott Rd., Floydville Rd.,** and **Rte. 189** links the next section which begins in East Granby at the former **Granby Station**. Heading up a slight incline, the trail passes the backyards of a few homes and then enjoys woodsy surroundings for the next mile to **Rte. 20** at a trailhead parking lot. The uphill pitch continues into **Newgate Wildlife Management Area** where white birch trees line the pavement, then flattens in a wooded swamp. It emerges on **Copper Hill Rd.** at another endpoint about 1.5 miles from Rte. 20 and 2.5 miles from Rte. 189.

The final developed section of the Farmington Valley Greenway is in Suffield and accessible from **Phelps Rd.** where a new pedestrian bridge spans the roadway. A newly paved surface extends southward for 0.9 miles through an area of farm fields, then reverts to gravel and eventually gets hindered by the presence of railroad ties. To the north,

76

the rail bed has a surface of crushed stone and follows the old canal for 0.6 miles to the state line where it enters a bog and continues with rougher conditions.

DRIVING DIRECTIONS:

To reach the Brickyard Rd. trailhead in Farmington from I-84, take Exit 39 and follow Rte. 4 west for 2.7 miles. Turn right on Brickyard Rd. and the parking lot is a mile ahead on the left.

To reach the Latimer La. trailhead in Simsbury, take Exit 50 from I-84 and follow Rte. 44 west for 9.5 miles. Turn right on Rte. 10 north and continue for 2.2 miles, then turn left on Latimer La. Look for the parking lot on the left.

To reach the Rte. 10/Rte. 315 trailhead in Simsbury, take Exit 40 and follow Rte. 20 west for 9.4 miles to Granby. Turn left on Rte. 10 south, continue for 4.3 miles, and look for the trailhead on the left after the intersection of Rte. 315.

To reach the Rte. 20 trailhead in East Granby, take Exit 40 from I-91 and follow Rte. 20 west for 8.2 miles. Park in the lot on the right at the Newgate Wildlife Management Area.

TOILET FACILITIES:

A toilet is located at the Rte. 10/Rte. 315 trailhead in Simsbury.

BIKE SHOPS:

Benidorm Bikes, 247 Albany Tpke., Canton, (860) 693-8891
Bicycle Cellar, 532 Hopmeadow St., Simsbury, (860) 658-1311
Biker's Edge, 465 N. Main St., Bristol, (860) 582-7770
Central Wheel, 62 Farmington Ave., Farmington, (860) 677-7010
Country Sports, 65 Albany Tpke., Canton, (860) 693-2267
Renaissance Cyclery, 49 W. Main St., Plainville, (860) 747-2909
Ski & Bike Market, 195 W. Main St., Avon, (860) 677-2186
Valley Bicycle, 10 Hartford Ave., Granby, (860) 653-6545

ADDITIONAL INFORMATION:

Farmington Valley Trails Council, PO Box 576, Tarriffville, CT 06081, http://members.aol.com/fvgreenway

Avon Recreation & Park Dept., 60 W. Main St., Avon, CT 06001, Tel. (860) 409-4332

Farmington Parks & Recreation Dept., 1 Monteith Dr., Farmington, CT 06032

Simsbury Parks & Recreation Dept., 933 Hopmeadow St., Simsbury, CT 06070, Tel. (860) 658-3255

12
Farmington River Trail
Farmington - Collinsville

length: 2 separate sections totaling 6.5 miles
surface: mostly pavement (some crushed stone)
terrain: gentle slopes

This new rail-trail follows the rapids of the Farmington River for much of the way and crosses an old trestle bridge at the mill village of Collinsville. The trail's two segments are not yet contiguous but will hopefully be joined soon.

BACKGROUND:

The Farmington River Trail follows a rail spur which was built in 1850 from the New Haven and Northampton Railroad. The line served Unionville, Burlington, and the burgeoning manufacturing operations at Collinsville, but its usefulness faded in the mid-1900's as times changed. The state's Dept. of Transportation eventually acquired the rail line and transferred management of the route to the Dept. of Environmental Protection in 1988 so that it could be used for recreation. Construction in 1999 and 2000 established two segments of the trail and more work is planned.

RULES OF THE TRAIL:

The Farmington River Trail attracts a steady stream of self-propelled traffic on fair weather weekend days so be prepared to share the pavement. Bicyclists should keep to the right side, ride at safe speeds, and yield to pedestrians. To avoid surprising others when passing from behind, give a friendly greeting or call "On your left!" well in advance.

Alcohol and motor vehicles are prohibited from the trail. Dogs must be leashed. The trail is open for use only during daylight hours.

ORIENTATION:

The trail presently exists in two parts. A 4.3-mile section runs from Rte. 4 in Farmington through Burlington to

Collinsville in Canton and a 2.2-mile section in Farmington runs between Rte. 177 and Red Oak Hill Rd. It is possible to join the two sections using about a mile of roads which include busy Rte. 4. Future construction will hopefully unite the two sections.

The 4.3 miles from Canton to Farmington get the most use but include a 0.4-mile on-road bike route along Arch St., a lightly traveled back road, and a 1.2-mile unpaved portion at the southern end.

The trail's developed sections have a wide surface of pavement, protective fencing at steep bankings, and well designed road crossings with crosswalks and signs. Trailhead parking is available at the junction of routes 4 and 179 in Burlington and at New Britain Ave. in Farmington.

TRAIL DESCRIPTION:

Starting at the Burlington trailhead parking lot near the junction of routes 4 and 179, face the trail and turn left, heading north toward Collinsville. The **Farmington River** flows over a rocky course on the right side of the trail while **Rte. 179** parallels at a higher elevation on the left. The 10-foot-wide paved surface provides easy rolling along the old rail bed, threading a tight course between the river and the road while clinging to the side of an everpresent slope. A faint uphill grade marks the next 2.3 miles to Collinsville.

The trail encounters 3 wooden bridges built across stream gullies in the first mile, continues past a second access point on Rte. 179, and passes an old power generating dam which creates a small waterfall in the river. The separated bike path ends at the intersection of Burlington Ave. and **Arch St.** at a sharp bend in the river, about 1.7 miles north of the parking lot.

Here a 0.4-mile bike route begins on a quiet, back road. Turn right on Arch St. and continue upstream along the river as it bends back to the left, then look for the trail to resume at a wooden ramp on the right side of the road. The ramp rises to join a trestle bridge over the Farmington River offering a view over the water and the nearby buildings of

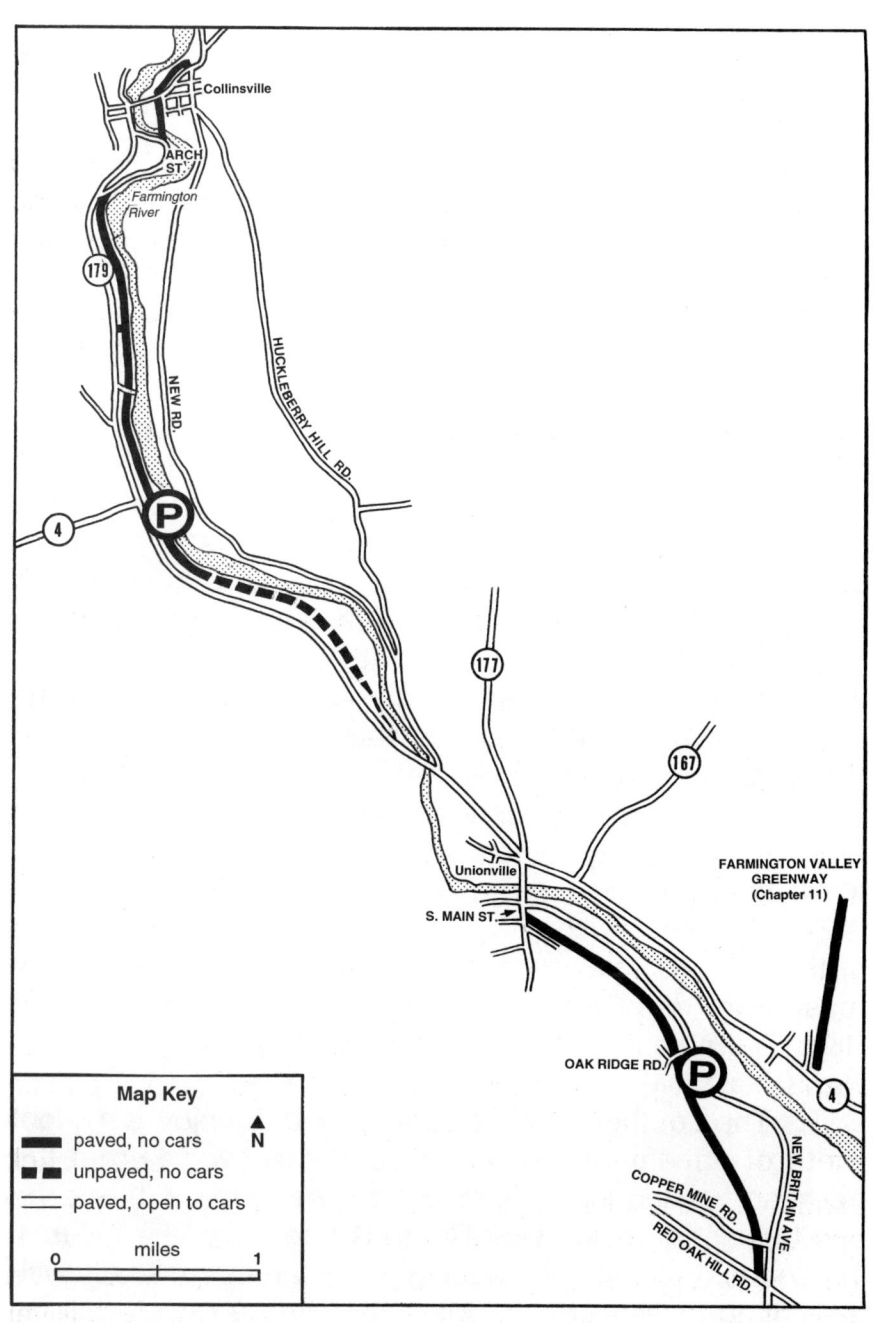

Collinsville

ARCH ST.

Farmington River

179

NEW RD.

HUCKLEBERRY HILL RD.

4

P

177

167

Unionville

S. MAIN ST.

FARMINGTON VALLEY
GREENWAY
(Chapter 11)

OAK RIDGE RD.

P

4

NEW BRITAIN AVE.

COPPER MINE RD.

RED OAK HILL RD.

Map Key

▲ N

━━ paved, no cars

▄ ▄ unpaved, no cars

══ paved, open to cars

0   miles   1

Collinsville, a mill village which grew to prominence as the home of the Collins Company, manufacturer of knives, axes, and other metal edge products. Several signs sit beside the trail's next half-mile offering historical information and old photographs of the village.

Descending the bridge on another ramp, the trail sneaks through a cluster of mill buildings which now house a variety of stores and small industries, passes a former depot building, then crosses Bridge St. (Rte. 179) at the 2.4-mile mark. Turning right, it continues beside the road for another third of a mile before ending near the intersection of Maple Ave. and River Rd.

Heading south from the Burlington trailhead parking lot, the trail has not been officially developed but is still passable for most cyclists. The trip begins on an old stretch of pavement which was once Rte. 4. This abandoned roadway follows the riverbank closely and lasts for about 0.4 miles where a smooth, firm surface of crushed stone continues along the rail bed and guides riders farther downstream beside more rapids. After another 0.4 miles, the trail leaves the edge of the water and remains close to the road, then crosses a residential driveway and becomes narrower. Overgrown conditions and a loose surface of crushed stone hamper the pedaling for the remaining third of a mile to **Rte. 4**.

Until construction is completed on the next segment of the rail bed, bicyclists must either detour using Rte. 4 (east) and then Rte. 177 (south) to reach the Farmington River Trail's southern section or park at the trailhead lot on New Britain Ave.

The southernmost 2.2 miles of trail enjoy a 12-foot width of pavement but no views of the river. From the trailhead parking lot on **New Britain Ave.**, follow the fence and trail uphill beside **Oak Ridge Rd.** to reach the rail-trail. Turning to the right and heading north, it runs for a mile with a slight downhill pitch to **S. Main St. (Rte. 177)** with split-rail fencing corralling the trail through an industrial area at the outskirts of **Unionville** where several depots and other railroad-era buildings are reminders of the trail's origins.

Turning to the left and heading south, the trail ventures for 1.2 miles through a mix of residential and wooded areas. Starting with a slight incline and eventually flattening, the trail crosses **Copper Mine Rd.** after 1 mile and then merges beside New Britain Ave. before ending at **Red Oak Hill Rd.**

DRIVING DIRECTIONS:

From I-84 take Exit 39 and follow signs for Rte. 4 west. To reach the New Britain Ave. trailhead parking lot in Farmington, follow Rte. 4 west for about 5.7 miles to Unionville, turn left on Rte. 177 south (S. Main St.), cross the Farmington River, then take the first left on New Britain Ave. Continue for 1.1 miles and look for the parking lot on the right, just after Oak Ridge Rd.

To reach the Burlington trailhead at the junction of routes 4 and 179, take Exit 39 from I-84 and follow Rte. 4 west for about 8.4 miles. Look for the parking lot on the right at the traffic signal where Rte. 4 turns left and Rte. 179 continues straight.

TOILET FACILITIES:

No toilets are provided.

BIKE SHOPS:

Benidorm Bikes, 247 Albany Tpke., Canton, (860) 693-8891
Bicycle Cellar, 532 Hopmeadow St., Simsbury, (860) 658-1311
Biker's Edge, 465 N. Main St., Bristol, (860) 582-7770
Central Wheel, 62 Farmington Ave., Farmington, (860) 677-7010
Country Sports, 65 Albany Tpke., Canton, (860) 693-2267
Renaissance Cyclery, 49 W. Main St., Plainville, (860) 747-2909
Ski & Bike Market, 195 W. Main St., Avon, (860) 677-2186

ADDITIONAL INFORMATION:

Farmington Valley Trails Council, PO Box 576, Tarriffville, CT 06081, http://members.aol.com/fvgreenway

13
Stratton Brook State Park
Simsbury

length: 2 sections totaling 1.9 miles
surface: stone dust
terrain: flat

This small, family-oriented state park has something for everyone: a swimming beach, fishing hole, picnic area, and for those who can't sit still, a pleasant stretch of rail-trail. A quieter, simpler alternative to the nearby Farmington Valley Greenway, Stratton Brook's peaceful bike path is a neighborhood favorite.

BACKGROUND:

This route originated in 1871 as the Connecticut Western Railroad which connected Hartford with the Hudson River. It later became part of the Central New England Railroad and then part of the New York, New Haven, and Hartford Railroad. Passenger service along this line was discontinued during the 1920's as automobile and bus travel gained popularity and freight service ended during the1930's in the Great Depression. The Civilian Conservation Corps (C.C.C.) pulled up the tracks in 1937 so that park visitors could enjoy the route.

Stratton Brook State Park's 145 acres were originally part of nearby Massacoe State Forest which was established in 1908. During its early years, the state forest served as a testing area for minimizing the risk of forest fires caused by the sparks of passing steam engines, a persistent problem at the time. Following the construction of a dam along Stratton Brook by the C.C.C. in 1933, the area saw increasing amounts of recreational use from a growing suburban population. A second pond was created in 1965 to keep pace with demand and today it ranks as the park's main attraction.

TRAIL POLICIES:

Bicyclists should plan to ride slowly in the area of the swimming and fishing ponds which can be busy with people on sunny weekends. Be especially careful in the presence of young children whose movements can be unpredictable. Keep to the right side, pass on the left after audibly signaling, and step off the trail when stopped. Remember that pedestrians have the right of way and bicyclists must yield.

Stratton Brook State Park is open to picnicking, swimming, and fishing (licence required). Alcohol is not permitted. Horses and motorized vehicles are prohibited from the trail. An admission fee is charged when entering the park by car during the summer season. The area is open from 8:00 AM to sunset.

ORIENTATION:

The bike path is aligned in the northeast-southwest direction and stretches for 3.3 miles from end to end. Near the middle of this distance, a 1.4-mile section follows Town Forest Rd. which is open to cars, although traffic is typically light. The remainder of the route is closed to cars.

Stratton Brook State Park is located toward the northeastern end of the trail and is the recommended starting point for bicyclists. The trail's stone dust surface is firm, smooth, and about 10 feet wide. Gates block vehicles from entering at road intersections, which are few.

TRAIL DESCRIPTION:

Approaching the bike path from the trailhead at **Stratton Brook State Park**, turn left and follow it in the northeasterly direction toward Simsbury. The trail soon leaves the lively area of the swimming pond and finds peace and quiet in the evergreen forest which encloses the rail bed on both sides. Tall white pines closely border the trail, shading it from summer heat and giving it a more natural look than many other rail-trails.

The trail follows **Stratton Brook** for the first third of a mile, then crosses a bridge over its flow and continues in a

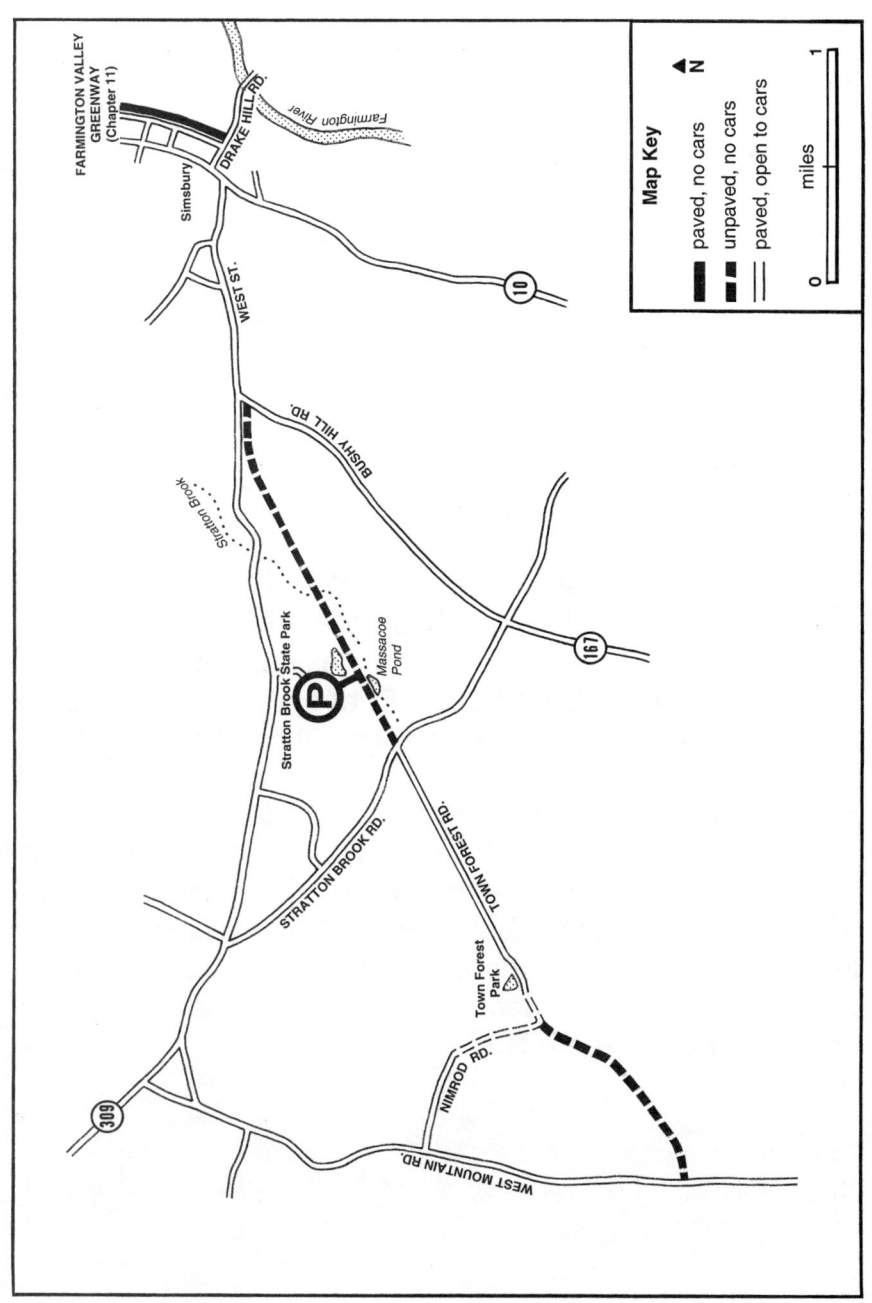

FARMINGTON VALLEY
GREENWAY
(Chapter 11)

Simsbury

DRAKE HILL RD.

Farmington River

WEST ST.

10

BUSHY HILL RD.

Stratton Brook

Stratton Brook State Park

P

Massacoe
Pond

167

STRATTON BROOK RD.

TOWN FOREST RD.

Town Forest
Park

NIMROD RD.

309

WEST MOUNTAIN RD.

Map Key

▬ paved, no cars

▬ ▬ unpaved, no cars

═ paved, open to cars

▲ N

0   miles   1

straight line course through a stand of hemlocks. After three quarters of a mile, the rail-trail's perfect line gives way to a gentle right-hand turn which lasts for another quarter mile to **Bushy Hill Rd. (Rte. 167)** where the trail ends.

Another rail-trail, the **Farmington Valley Greenway** (Chapter 11), passes through the nearby center of Simsbury on its partially completed route between Farmington and Suffield. To find it, turn left on Bushy Hill Rd., then immediately right on **West St.** (Rte. 167) and continue down the hill. At the bottom, turn left on **Rte. 10** and then right on **Drake Hill Rd.** and look for the trail ahead on the left beside Iron Horse Blvd.

Heading in the opposite direction from the Stratton Brook State Park trailhead, the bike path ventures toward the southwest horizon along the same straight corridor. It passes the banks of **Massacoe Pond**, a popular fishing hole, then hits a gate beside **Stratton Brook Rd.** after a quarter-mile. Crossing the street, the rail-trail continues on **Town Forest Rd.** for the next 1.4 miles passing a parking lot and small pond at **Town Forest Park** on the right side along the way. The road's paved surface changes to gravel near this point.

Town Forest Rd. ends beside a ball field at a sharp, right-hand turn where **Nimrod Rd.** begins. The rail-trail continues straight at this intersection, rising on a slight but noticeable slope with a left-hand bend and slipping between two residential neighborhoods. Tall white pines line the trail along this last leg. A metal gate marks the end of the public trail at **West Mountain Rd.**

DRIVING DIRECTIONS:

From I-91 take Exit 40 and follow Rte. 20 west for 9.4 miles to Granby. Turn left on Rte. 10 south and continue for 6.4 miles to Simsbury, then turn right on Rte. 167 south and drive for 0.8 miles. Continue straight on Rte. 309 west for 0.9 miles to the park entrance on the left.

From I-84 take Exit 50 and follow Rte. 44 west for 9.5 miles. Turn right on Rte. 10 north and drive for 3.8 miles to Simsbury, turn left on Rte. 167 south and continue for 0.8 miles, then follow Rte. 309 west for 0.9 miles. Look for the park entrance on the left.

TOILET FACILITIES:

Toilets are available at Stratton Brook State Park during the summer season.

BIKE SHOPS:

Benidorm Bikes, 247 Albany Tpke., Canton, (860) 693-8891
Bicycle Cellar, 532 Hopmeadow St., Simsbury, (860) 658-1311
Country Sports, 65 Albany Tpke., Canton, (860) 693-2267

ADDITIONAL INFORMATION:

Stratton Brook State Park, c/o Penwood State Park, 57 Gun Mill Rd., Bloomfield, CT 06002, (860) 242-1158

Connecticut Dept. of Environmental Protection, 79 Elm St., Hartford, CT 06106-5127, Tel. (860) 424-3200, http://dep.state.ct.us

14
MDC Reservoir
Canton, Burlington

length: 3 miles
surface: paved
terrain: one road is flat, the other is sloped

These forgotten stretches of pavement escape the sights and sounds of nearby civilization and offer a smaller and much quieter alternative to the MDC's West Hartford facility. Rough pavement and accumulated sand make in-line skating inadvisable.

BACKGROUND:

A special act of the Connecticut General Assembly sparked the construction of the Nepaug Reservoir during the years 1911 to 1916. In order to expand Hartford's water supply system, the city's water authority purchased all of the properties in the flood zone as well as the necessary surrounding acreage and built two large dams to contain the reservoir. At the time, the project ranked as the greatest engineering feat for a water supply in New England. The tributary waters of the Nepaug River, Clear Brook, and Phelps Brook supply the reservoir with spring-fed run-off from the bordering hills.

Creation of the reservoir required the evacuation of the village of Nepaug, a settlement of small farms dating from the late 1700's. It forced the relocation or destruction of all buildings within the flood zone and surrounding area which included 22 houses as well as the local school and a church. The graves of Nepaug's two cemeteries were moved to nearby Collinsville.

TRAIL POLICIES:

The Metropolitan District Commission (MDC) is a state-chartered organization and manages the property for Hartford's water supply. Recreational use of the area is limited to the two routes described in this chapter and visitors must adhere to the area's relatively strict regulations. Patrol officers enforce the regulations and issue citations to violators.

Bicyclists are requested to wear helmets, ride at a safe speed, and yield to pedestrians. When approaching others from behind, give a friendly warning to avoid startling them. Use of roads other than Torrington Ave. and Clear Brook Rd. is forbidden and venturing off these roads into surrounding areas is considered trespassing.

Dogs must be leashed at all times. The MDC cautions visitors not to block trailhead gates when parking since work crews and emergency vehicles always need access. The area is open from dawn to dusk.

ORIENTATION:

Two paved, car-free routes are available for recreational use at the Nepaug Reservoir. Torrington Ave. is a mile-long portion of roadway along the northern shoreline offering the mildest slopes, smoothest pavement, and several good views over the water. At the southern shoreline, Clear Brook Rd. measures two miles in length, has bigger hills, rougher pavement, and a more isolated location.

Roadside parking is permitted at the gated endpoints of each road. Other than the metal gates blocking vehicle entry and the pavement itself, no other amenities are provided.

TRAIL DESCRIPTIONS:

Starting at the western end of **Torrington Ave.** at the intersection of **Rte. 202**, visitors enjoy a view over a small meadow to the open waters of **Nepaug Reservoir** as they leave the trailhead gate. Curving to the left, the road parallels the shoreline on a side slope above the water, which is visible through the trees. A slight downhill grade eases the pedaling until the 0.4-mile mark where the pavement turns abruptly to the right and emerges on the 600-foot-long **Nepaug Dam** with another excellent view over

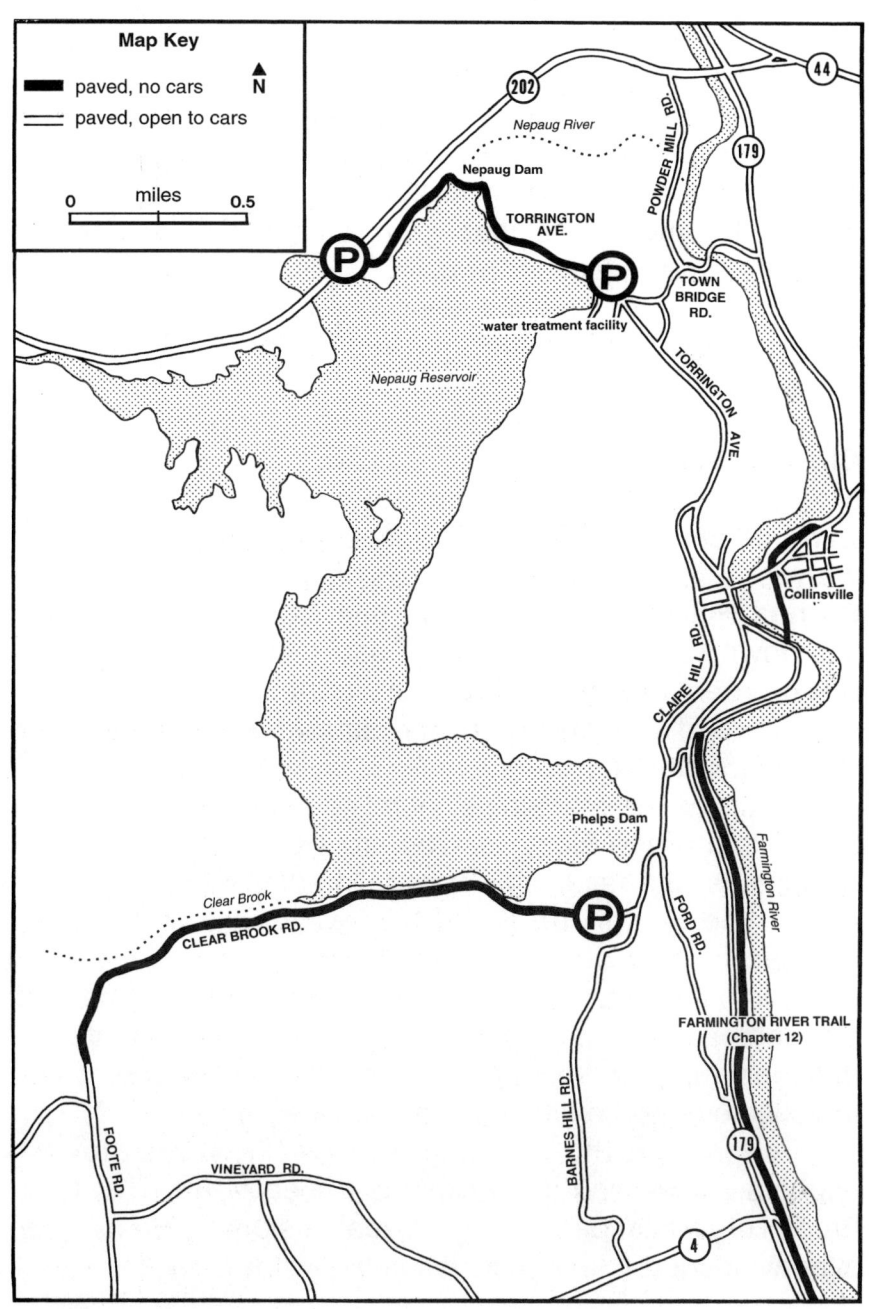

Map Key

- **paved, no cars** (thick line)
- paved, open to cars (thin line)

N

miles
0 — 0.5

202

Nepaug River

Nepaug Dam

TORRINGTON AVE.

POWDER MILL RD.

44

179

TOWN BRIDGE RD.

water treatment facility

Nepaug Reservoir

TORRINGTON AVE.

CLAIRE HILL RD.

Collinsville

Phelps Dam

Clear Brook

CLEAR BROOK RD.

FORD RD.

Farmington River

FARMINGTON RIVER TRAIL
(Chapter 12)

179

FOOTE RD.

VINEYARD RD.

BARNES HILL RD.

4

the water. The dam's crescent-shaped concrete structure forms a dramatic spillway for the reservoir's outflow which drops 130 feet into the **Nepaug River**.

The road crosses the top of the dam and enters the woods on the other side. Rising on a gentle incline, it continues paralleling the shoreline at a distance while curving through a corridor in the forest. The eastern gate appears at the 1-mile mark near an access road for the Nepaug Water Treatment Facility. Here Torrington Ave. is open to car traffic and tips downward for 1.2 miles to reach the village of Collinsville and the **Farmington River Tr.** (Chapter 12).

Alone at the southern end of the reservoir, 2-mile **Clear Brook Rd.** has a more isolated feel and noticeably older pavement. An abundance of pot holes and cracks warrants caution from cyclists especially when descending the road's long slopes. Beginning near the intersection of **Barnes Hill Rd.** at the eastern end, the road immediately tilts downhill from the trailhead gate and follows a row of larch trees along the remains of a few stone walls, reminders of the time when the surrounding acreage was cleared for farming.

It joins the reservoir's shoreline after a quarter-mile at the bottom of the slope, curves around a small cove, then straightens with relatively flat pedaling until the 1-mile mark. At this point an uphill grade develops and the road approaches the sound of **Clear Brook** which it follows up a valley into the reservation's protected woodlands. The pitch steepens as it climbs beside the brook then moderates as the road turns southward and reaches its endpoint at a metal gate near the intersection of **Foote Rd.**

Although the Farmington River Tr. (Chapter 12) appears on the map to be close to the eastern end of Clear Brook Rd., it is separated by a sizeable slope. The river lies over two hundred feet in elevation below the reservoir.

DRIVING DIRECTIONS:

To reach the Torrington Ave. trailhead off Rte. 202, take Exit 50 from I-84 and follow Rte. 44 west for 15 miles. Turn left on Rte. 202 west and continue for 1.5 miles. Look for the trailhead on the left before the reservoir.

To reach the Torrington Ave. trailhead near the water treatment facility, take Exit 50 from I-84 and follow Rte. 44 west for 15 miles. Turn left on Rte. 202 west, continue a short distance across Rte. 179, then take the next left on Powder Mill Rd. Continue for 0.6 miles to the end, turn right on Town Bridge Rd. and drive for another 0.3 miles to the end, then turn right on Torrington Ave. Park at the end being careful not to block access to the gate.

To reach the Clear Brook Rd. trailhead near Barnes Hill Rd., take Exit 39 from I-84 and follow signs for Rte. 4 west. From the first traffic signal, drive for 7.7 miles on Rte. 4 west to a traffic signal where Rte. 179 north intersects. Turn left and continue on Rte. 4 west for another half-mile, then turn right on Barnes Hill Rd. Drive for another 1.3 miles, then turn hard left on Clear Brook Rd. Park beside the gate being careful not to block access.

TOILET FACILITIES:

No toilets are provided.

BIKE SHOPS:

Benidorm Bikes, 247 Albany Tpke., Canton, (860) 693-8891
Country Sports, 65 Albany Tpke., Canton, (860) 693-2267

ADDITIONAL INFORMATION:

Metropolitan District Commission, PO Box 800, Hartford, CT 06142-0800, Tel. (860) 278-7850
web: www.themdc.com

15
MDC Reservoirs
West Hartford

length: 13 miles
surface: about half paved, half gravel
terrain: varies from gently rolling to hilly

Greater Hartford's favorite playground, this 3,000-acre parkland is an oasis for bicyclists, mountain bikers, in-line skaters, walkers, and runners. The gated roads roll and curve through a scenic landscape of lakes and forest.

BACKGROUND:

The Metropolitan District Commission (MDC) is a state-chartered organization and manages the property for Hartford's water supply and for passive recreation. The 3,000-acre tract has been used as a public water supply since 1867 and its trails, woods, and scenic views have been drawing recreational visitors since that time. Today it is one of the Hartford area's largest open space areas and its network of gated roads and trails are a year-round attraction for many forms of outdoor recreation.

RULES OF THE TRAIL:

The MDC imposes a relatively strict set of rules in order to protect the watershed and to provide safety for visitors. Bicyclists are required to wear helmets, and in-line skaters are required to wear helmets as well as knee, elbow, and wrist protection. Bikers and in-liners are asked to show respect for others by traveling in the designated bike lane (where it exists), stepping to the side when stopped, and using extra caution when in the presence of children. Bicycling is not permitted on the bankings which line the many dams and impoundments and on trails that are marked with signs reading No Bikes.

The park is open from 8:00 AM until 8:00 PM or one half-hour after sunset, whichever is earlier. Dogs must be leashed at all times and owners must remove their pet's wastes. Swimming and fishing in the reservoirs is not permitted.

ORIENTATION:

Display maps with "You are here" designations are stationed at a couple of points along the most heavily traveled routes but few other signs are present to guide newcomers. The 6 miles of paved roads explore the area of the reservoirs and center on a popular one-way loop which is identifiable by a bike lane painted on its surface. About 7 miles of unpaved roads venture farther into the woods and have less usage, fewer signs and navigational aids, and bigger hills.

TRAIL DESCRIPTIONS:

The highlight for most cyclists is the scenic 3.4-mile paved loop which starts at the main trailhead parking lot. Since it is one-way for bicyclists and must be ridden in the clockwise direction, follow **Reservoir Rd.** southwest past several large, earthen impoundments in an area of lawns. The paved surface arcs to the right and passes a yellow gate after 0.4 miles at the edge of woods. Here a painted bike lane restricts cyclists to the right side.

The road climbs a slope after this point, turns northward at the top, and rolls along flat ground on a stretch known as **Red Rd.** Near the 1-mile mark it rises on a second slope to a dam containing **Reservoir 3**, then circles the southern tip of the reservoir and continues northward along the shoreline for almost a mile of flat riding, passing Middle Rd. and Dyke Pond Rd. along the way.

The loop turns eastward at **Reservoir 2** and encounters a series of small, rolling hills and numerous intersections. The painted bike lane guides riders through the junctions, descending at first on **Causeway Rd.**, forking left onto **Northwest Rd.**, and turning right on **Reservoir Rd. Extension**. After circling the northern end of **Reservoir 5**, the loop returns southward past the end of Canal Rd. at the 2.6-mile mark. It finishes with a flat, 0.8-mile leg along the

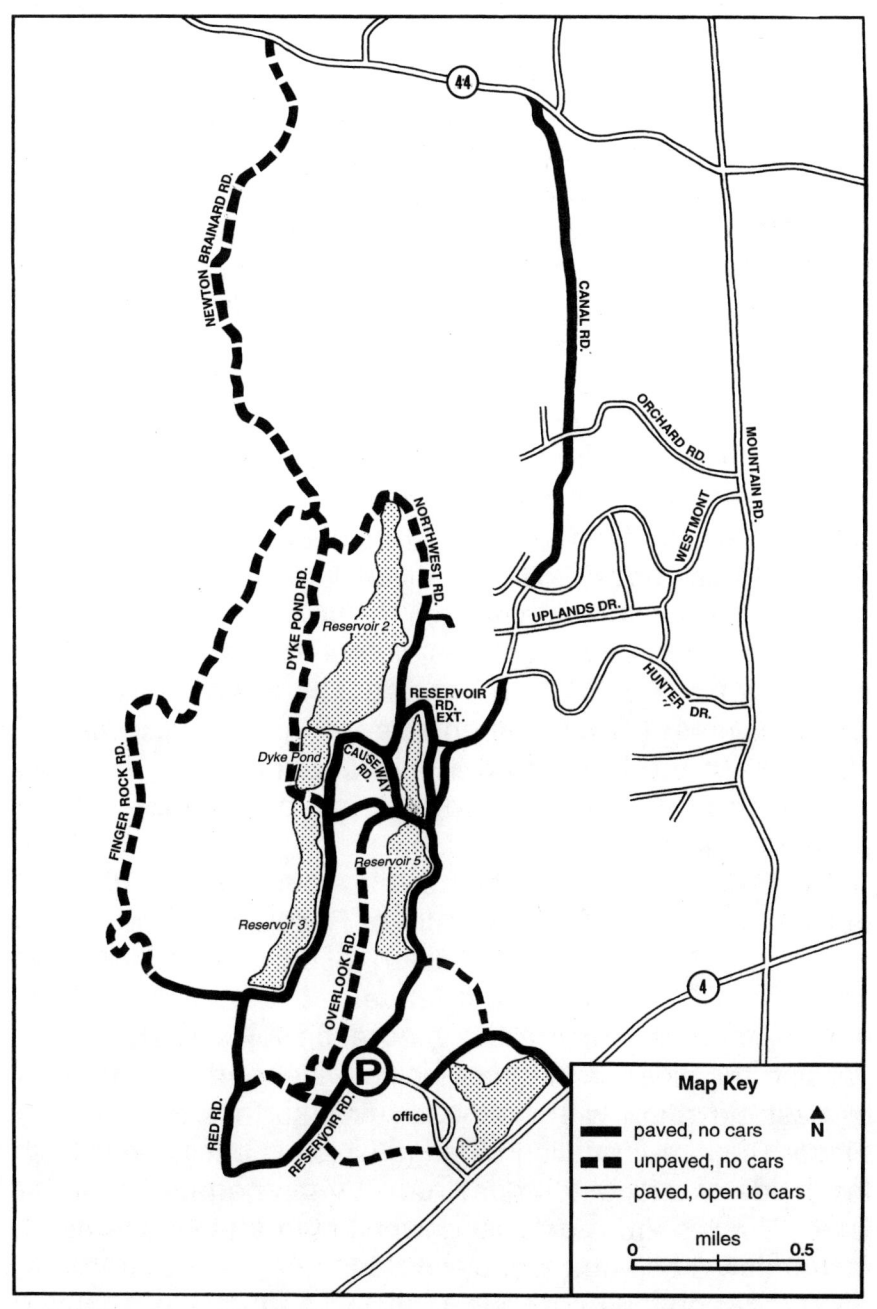

NEWTON BRAINARD RD.

44

CANAL RD.

ORCHARD RD.

MOUNTAIN RD.

WESTMONT

UPLANDS DR.

HUNTER DR.

NORTHWEST RD.

DYKE POND RD.

Reservoir 2

RESERVOIR RD. EXT.

Dyke Pond

CAUSEWAY RD.

FINGER ROCK RD.

Reservoir 5

Reservoir 3

OVERLOOK RD.

4

P

RED RD.

RESERVOIR RD.

office

Map Key

N

━━━ paved, no cars

▬ ▬ ▬ unpaved, no cars

——— paved, open to cars

miles

0   0.5

shore of Reservoir 5 with frequent views over the water.

Middle Rd. and Causeway Rd. bisect this loop with slightly shorter alternatives. Both roads descend toward the east and send riders across Reservoir 5 on an earthen causeway.

Lesser-traveled **Canal Rd.** offers a 2.3-mile spur with a mostly flat course on the bed of a former canal, although a short distance at the midsection is open to cars. Heading northward from Reservoir 5, it starts with an uphill and then flattens with a curving route which slips through several residential neighborhoods on a narrow strip of public land. At the half-mile mark it is open to cars for a third of a mile but the traffic is very light. Car-free pavement resumes for the remaining 1.5 miles to **Rte. 44** (Albany Tpke.) where an abrupt drop to the roadway deserves extreme caution. Biking along this high speed, four-lane road is discouraged.

Gravel roads provide additional options although their hills tend to be larger and their surfaces can be rough in spots. **Overlook Rd.** occupies high ground above the main parking lot at Reservoir 5 and requires a strenuous climb which is most gradual when ridden from north to south. Once on top, riders enjoy a mile of gently rolling slopes before they descend a steeper, rougher slope at the southern end of the road.

Finger Rock Rd. holds the biggest hills. It starts from Red Rd. at the southern tip of Reservoir 3 and climbs in switchbacks for almost a mile on a surface that alternates between old pavement and gravel. The steepest points have washouts which are a hindrance for cyclists. After passing prominent rock outcroppings, the road flattens at its highest elevation with a smooth, firm surface and passes Finger Rock, a formation of ledge which is easily noticed at the inside of a long, left-hand turn. At the northern end, the final 1.2 miles are a gradual downhill with a few parts being moderately steep and slightly eroded.

Two options continue from the northern terminus of Finger Rock Rd. **Newton Brainard Rd.** heads northward for 1.5 miles to Rte. 44 through rolling, forested terrain which includes one significant downhill with a loose surface near the 1-mile mark. Aside from the sight of a powerline and a gas pipeline, it offers purely natural surroundings in one of the more remote corners of the park.

Returning to the south, mile-long **Dyke Pond Rd.** curves through an area of rock outcroppings before descending gradually along a side-hill to **Dyke Pond** and the pavement of Red Rd. Along the way it intersects **Northwest Rd.**, also a mile in length, which drops more quickly for a third of a mile, rounds the northern tip of Reservoir 2, and returns through gentle terrain to the paved routes.

DRIVING DIRECTIONS:
From I-84 take Exit 39. At the first traffic signal, turn right on Rte. 4 east and measure 2.3 miles, then turn left at the park entrance. To reach the main parking lot, follow the paved road past the office building to the end.

TOILET FACILITIES:
Portable toilets are located at the parking lot.

BIKE SHOPS:
Benidorm Bikes, 247 Albany Tpke., Canton, (860) 693-8891
Bloomfield Bicycle, 5 Seneca Rd., Bloomfield, (860) 242-9884
Central Wheel, 62 Farmington Ave., Farmington, (860) 677-7010
Country Sports, 65 Albany Tpke., Canton, (860) 693-2267
Newington Bicycle, 1030 Main St., Newington, (860) 667-0857
Renaissance Cyclery, 49 W. Main St., Plainville, (860) 747-2909
Ski & Bike Market, 195 W. Main St., Avon, (860) 677-2186
Wethersfield Bicycle, 212 Church St., Wethersfield, (860) 563-3000

ADDITIONAL INFORMATION:
Metropolitan District Commission, P.O. Box 800, Hartford, CT 06142-0800,Tel. (860) 278-7850
web: www.themdc.com

16
Penwood State Park
Bloomfield

length: 3.7-mile loop
surface: old pavement (not suited for in-line skating)
terrain: hilly

In addition to popular hiking and mountain biking trails, Penwood has a car-free loop for bicycling. The forested route encounters some long, gradual slopes and treats riders with a few spectacular views.

BACKGROUND:

Curtis H. Veeder gifted this land to the state in 1944 with the hope that others could enjoy its natural beauty as he did. The 787-acre park had been his summer estate and was named Penwood for the fact that Mr. Veeder had family roots in Pennsylvania and because the name Veeder is Dutch for pen.

Veeder was both a successful industrialist and an avid outdoorsman and these interests spurred him to engineer and build many of the woodland trails and roads that park visitors enjoy today. Mowed lawns and a picnic area occupy his former homesite.

RULES OF THE TRAIL:

Bicyclists should keep to the right side and give a warning before passing others to avoid startling them. Since there are many curves and slopes, ride at a safe speed and be ready to share the road with other cyclists and walkers.

In addition, bicyclists should be aware of the unique center drains which exist along much of the road. The drains were conceived and engineered by Mr. Veeder and effectively shed rainwater but unfortunately resemble potholes in the middle of the road. They are painted yellow for visibility.

The road's aging asphalt surface also deserves caution. Bumps, cracks, and other imperfections are often obscured by fallen leaves so pedal cautiously.

Penwood's distinctive topography assists visitors in tracking their location. The park's road forms a thin loop around a ridgeline which runs in the north-south direction between Lake Louise in the north and Gale Pond in the south. The road's highest point is near the Cedar Ridge Overlook and its lowest is the Shadow Pond parking lot near the ranger station.

Few signs exist to guide visitors but few are needed since the road's pavement forms a self-contained loop with few opportunities for wrong turns. The pavement measures 10-12 feet wide and is in poor condition in places.

TRAIL DESCRIPTION:

Park Rd. forms a scenic, 3.5-mile loop which offers a taste of Penwood's dramatic terrain. Designed and constructed under the guidance of Mr. Veeder, the road ascends and descends sizeable hills and, for much of its distance, follows a shelf of land cut into the hillside where rock and ledge rise on one side and the slope falls away on the other.

Following the loop in the counter-clockwise direction from the **Gale Pond** trailhead parking lot beside **Rte. 185**, begin on the 1.3-mile access road to the ranger station. The narrow road is open to two-way car traffic, posted at 10 m.p.h., and gets little use. Follow it along the boundary fence beside Gale Pond, first around a right-hand turn and then to a left-hand turn (at 0.2 miles) then fork right on an unpaved bike path.

Paralleling the road, this bike path measures 6-8 feet wide and has a surface of stone dust for much of the way. It starts with a mostly downhill course along the park boundary and the backyards of several homes, then widens at the 0.6-mile mark where it merges with an old road and continues past a few hayfields. The path narrows on a short detour

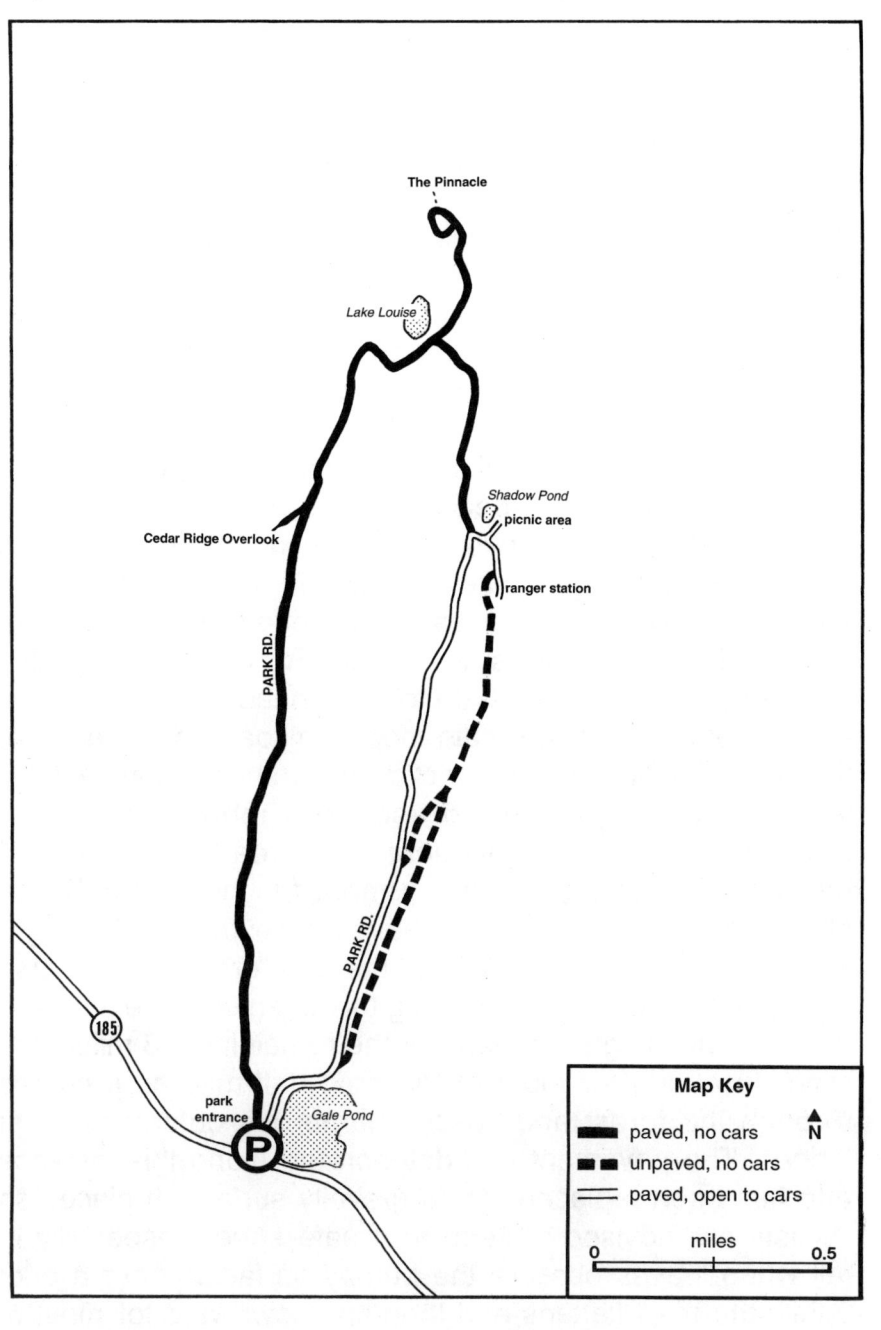

The Pinnacle

Lake Louise

Cedar Ridge Overlook

Shadow Pond
picnic area

ranger station

PARK RD.

PARK RD.

185

park
entrance

P

Gale Pond

Map Key

N

▬▬▬ paved, no cars

■ ■ ■ unpaved, no cars

═══ paved, open to cars

miles

0   0.5

around maintenance buildings at the **ranger station** and ends in an area of lawns nearby, 1.4 miles from the Rte. 185 trailhead.

Turn left on the pavement at the ranger station and ride uphill past the **Shadow Pond** parking lot to the edge of the woods, then turn right on the gated road to continue the Park Rd. loop. Cut into the side of the hill, the road climbs on a steady grade for a half-mile to **Lake Louise**, a small pond perched in a saddle on the ridgeline where many riders will want to pause to catch their breath and admire the view. The pond's natural shoreline is dominated by boggy plants and is easily visible from a wooden boardwalk which begins beside the road.

A short side trip forks to the right at this point. A third of a mile in length, this dead end road climbs quickly to the site of Curtis Veeder's cabin beneath **the Pinnacle**, a rock outcropping with a great view. It forks in a loop which circles the clearing of the former cabin and offers a western vista through the trees near its high point. For a better view, hike uphill on the blue-blazed path to the Pinnacle.

Returning to the main loop, the road continues over flat ground in a westerly direction for a short distance, then turns south and begins to ascend a long slope with a crumbling surface of pavement. The road climbs for 0.4 miles, then tops the hill at a turnout for the **Cedar Ridge Overlook** where a short, unpaved side trail on the right leads uphill to a panorama of the western horizon. Use appropriate caution when visiting this open cliff face.

Continuing southward for the remaining 1.3 miles, the road descends for most of the next half-mile as it curves through the forest and passes numerous outcroppings of ledge. The pavement has deteriorated along this distance and has been replaced with a gravelly surface in places so cyclists are advised to keep to a safe speed, especially in fall when leaves obscure the bumpy surface. After a brief uphill, the road flattens and then tips downward for most of the last half-mile to the parking lot at Gale Pond.

DRIVING DIRECTIONS:

From I-84 take Exit 50 and follow Rte. 44 west for 2.5 miles. Turn right (north) on Rte. 189 and drive for 0.8 miles, then turn left (west) on Rte. 185 and continue for 5 miles. Look for the park entrance on the right and park in the lot just ahead or continue for 1.3 miles to the Shadow Pond lot near the ranger station.

TOILET FACILITIES:

Toilets are located at the Shadow Pond parking lot.

BIKE SHOPS:

Bicycle Cellar, 532 Hopmeadow St., Simsbury, (860) 658-1311
Bloomfield Bicycle, 5 Seneca Rd., Bloomfield, (860) 242-9884
Ski & Bike Market, 195 W. Main St., Avon, (860) 677-2186

ADDITIONAL INFORMATION:

Penwood State Park, 57 Gun Mill Rd., Bloomfield, CT 06002, Tel. (860) 242-1158
web: http://dep.state.ct.us

17

Charter Oak Landing, Great River Park
Hartford, East Hartford

length: 4.5 miles
surface: mostly pavement
terrain: flat

A greenbelt at the front steps of the city, this cluster of waterfront parks has transformed the banks of the Connecticut into a scenic recreational asset. While some connections remain to be made, the revitalized areas are a great find for city-bound pedalers.

BACKGROUND:

Hartford's waterfront had suffered during the city's growth. The arrival of the railroad in 1835 separated the riverbank from the city, the construction of a floodwall in 1942 blocked the river from view, and the completion of I-91 in 1962 added an impenetrable barrier.

The "Riverfront Recapture" effort to reclaim public access and restore the city's connection to the river started in 1981 and continues today. The first portions of the so-called riverwalk system were acheived when the city of Hartford completed Charter Oak Landing in 1989 and East Hartford opened Great River Park in 1990. The initiative reached a major milestone in 1999 when Riverfront Plaza, Founders Bridge Promenade, and State St. Landing were dedicated. In the shadow of the city skyline, paved trails, outdoor performance areas, boat landings, and picnic areas now invite people to enjoy the river and its banks.

The Metropolitan District Commission (MDC) and Riverfront Recapture, Inc. manage and maintain the area.

TRAIL POLICIES:

The proximity of the city draws lots of pedestrian use so bicyclists are cautioned to pedal slowly. Keep to the right side, pass on the left, and give a friendly warning when approaching others from behind to avoid startling them.

Pets must be leashed and pet wastes must be removed. The area is open during daylight hours.

ORIENTATION:

The Connecticut River is a unifying landmark which is visible from all parts of the paved trail network and divides the trails on the west bank (Hartford) from those on the east bank (East Hartford). Crossing the river is possible on bike/pedestrian pathways of three highway bridges but involves climbing and descending long stairways so many cyclists will choose to explore either one side or the other.

The riding on the western side is not yet completely paved and encounters two challenging segments for bicycling. Many points along the trails are subject to flooding during wet periods so plan your visit accordingly.

TRAIL DESCRIPTIONS:

The longest stretch of contiguous bike path lies on the east bank at **Great River Park**. Landscaped grounds lend a relaxing atmosphere to the park and its riverbank location provides a good view of the Hartford skyline.

Heading north from the parking lot near the boat ramp, the paved trail runs for 0.7 miles. It begins by following a row of decorative lamp poles along a corridor of lawn and shade trees. A 30' flood wall rises on the right side and protects the surrounding neighborhood from periodic flooding while the **Connecticut River** is visible through the trees on the left. After a third of a mile the trail arcs around the base of an apartment building and then passes underneath **Founders Bridge** (**Rte. 2**) where a stairway climbs to a bike/pedestrian pathway across the river.

Continuing northward, the trail follows more lamp poles to an area of benches overlooking the water and then veers uphill on a gradual slope to the **Bulkeley Bridge** and the roar of **I-84**. Here two short side trails branch to East River Dr.: one heads south along the top of the floodwall and the other runs east along the Exit 53 off-ramp.

Heading south from the Great River Park parking lot,

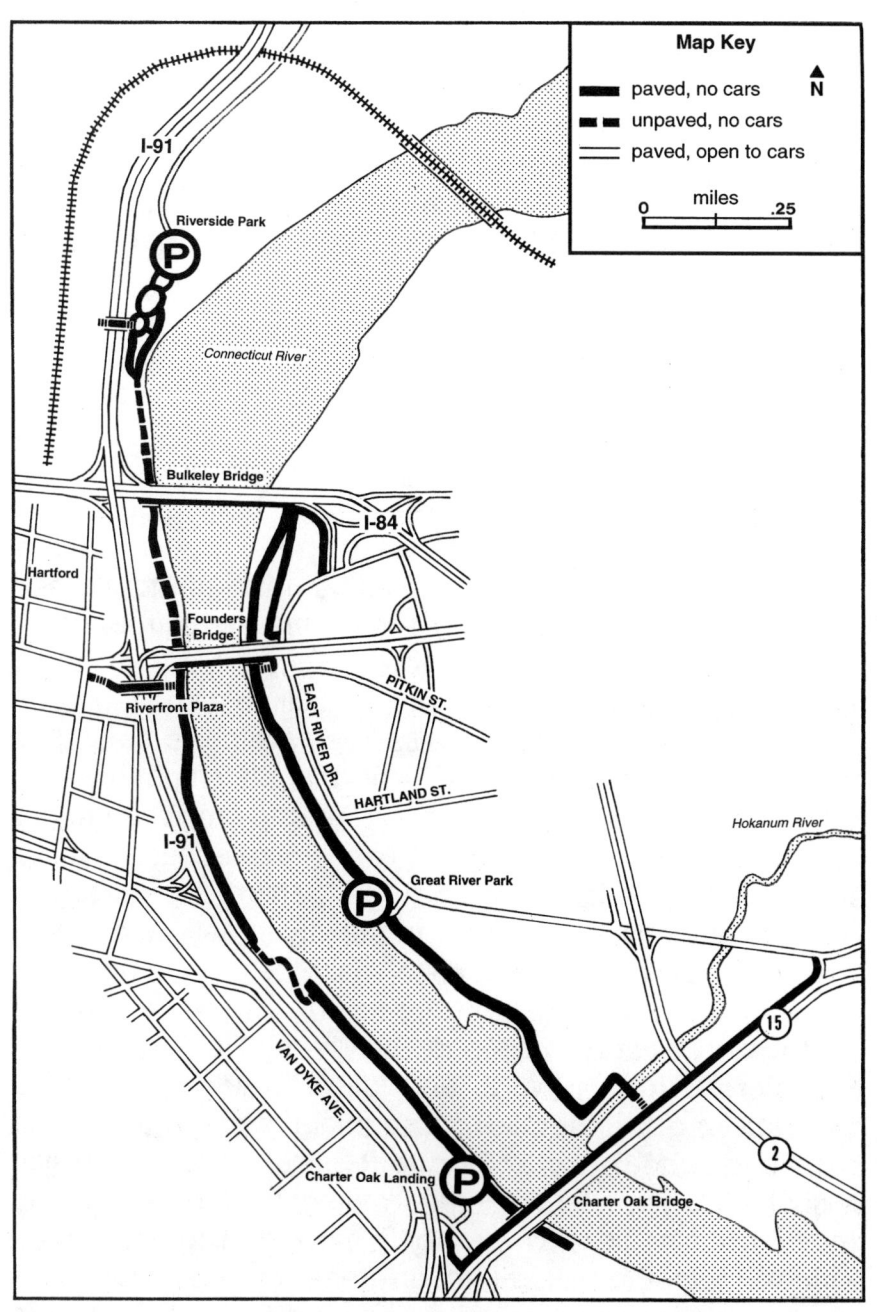

Map Key

N

━━━ paved, no cars

▬ ▬ unpaved, no cars

─── paved, open to cars

miles
0   .25

I-91

Riverside Park

Connecticut River

Bulkeley Bridge

I-84

Hartford

Founders Bridge

PITKIN ST.

Riverfront Plaza

EAST RIVER DR.

HARTLAND ST.

Hokanum River

I-91

Great River Park

15

VAN DYKE AVE.

2

Charter Oak Landing

Charter Oak Bridge

the trail offers another three quarters of a mile of quieter scenery. Removed from the sights and sounds of nearby civilization, the smooth pathway meanders beside a natural border of woods lined with more lamp poles and a few benches overlooking the river. Near the end, the trail turns upstream beside the **Hokanum River**.

After crossing the Hokanum on a small bridge, the trail ends at the foot of a stairway below the **Charter Oak Bridge** (**Rte. 15**) which offers a mile of bike/pedestrian pathway between **East River Dr.** on the east bank and **Van Dyke Ave.** on the west bank. Although it requires climbing several flights of stairs, the bridge rewards cyclists with a grand view over the river.

Charter Oak Landing occupies the western shoreline with lawns, picnic tables, toilets, a playground, and parking lot. A half-mile of paved pathway traces the riverbank from the Charter Oak Bridge upstream to the end of the landscaped park, then a quarter-mile of rough dirt road continues northward. Follow it along the embankment below I-91, turn left where it forks, and climb a short, eroded slope to reach a paved access road which is closed to regular traffic. Heading straight on this pavement, cyclists top a small hill with a view of the river and then drop to the water's edge at Hartford's **Riverfront Plaza** about 1.2 miles north of the Charter Oak Bridge. Here a pedestrian overpass bridges I-91 to connect the city streets with a boat landing and outdoor performance space beside the river.

It is possible to venture farther northward using another unpaved road along the river. Pass under the **Founders Bridge** (**Rte. 2**) and follow it along a concrete floodwall for a quarter-mile to a segment of paved trail which loops under the **Bulkeley Bridge** (**I-84**) at a low point which is subject to flooding. A metal railing borders this paved trail. The asphalt ends after only a tenth of a mile but an earthen footpath snakes through trees for another quarter-mile to reach a small network of paved trails at **Riverside Park**, 1.9 miles north of the Charter Oak Bridge. The park's shady grounds, picnic area, and playground make an inviting place to stop and rest.

DRIVING DIRECTIONS:

Great River Park from I-84 westbound: Take Exit 54 and follow Rte. 2 west toward downtown Hartford. Take Exit 3, turn left on Darlin St. at the end of the ramp, then turn left on East River Dr. The parking lot is 0.8 miles ahead on the right.

Great River Park from I-84 eastbound: Take Exit 53 and follow signs for East River Dr. Turn right off the ramp and continue on East River Dr. for 0.7 miles to the parking lot on the right.

Charter Oak Landing from I-91 northbound: Take Exit 27 and turn left (north) on Brainard Rd. After 0.8 miles turn left on Reserve Rd. and continue for a half-mile to the park entrance on the right.

Charter Oak Landing from I-91 southbound: Take Exit 27 and turn left off the ramp on Airport Rd. Turn left on Brainard Rd. and drive for 0.7 miles, turn left on Reserve Rd. and continue for a half-mile to the park entrance on the right.

Riverside Park: Take Exit 33 from I-91 and turn east on Jennings Rd. Turn right (south) on Leibert Rd. and look for the park entrance 0.4 miles ahead on the left.

TOILET FACILITIES:

Toilets are located at Great River Park, Charter Oak Landing, and Riverside Park.

BIKE SHOPS:

Bicycles East, 2333 Main St., Glastonbury, (860) 659-0114
Bloomfield Bicycle, 5 Seneca Rd., Bloomfield, (860) 242-9884
E-Trans, 1026 Main St., East Hartford, (860) 289-8485
Newington Bicycle, 1030 Main St., Newington, (860) 667-0857
Pig Iron Bicycle Works, 38 Addison Rd., Glastonbury,
　　(860) 659-8808
Wethersfield Bicycle, 212 Church St., Wethersfield, (860) 563-3000

ADDITIONAL INFORMATION:

Riverfront Recapture, Inc., 1 Hartford Sq. West, Hartford, CT 06106-1984

Metropolitan District Commission (MDC), P.O. Box 800, Hartford, CT 06142-0800, Tel. (860) 278-7850
web: www.themdc.com

18
Windsor River Trail
Windsor

length: 1.4 miles
surface: paved
terrain: flat

Located at the town center, this is a convenient source of car-free pavement for locals and a trail that is well suited for in-line skating and biking with small children. The curvey trail features easy conditions and entirely natural surroundings along the shady banks of the Farmington River but several low-lying points could become impassible during periods of river flooding.

BACKGROUND:

The town of Windsor began creating this trail in 1993 with its engineering department managing the project. The trail utilizes town-owned lands as well as an abandoned public road dating from Colonial times known as Rowland Lane, once the main route along the Connecticut River from Hartford to points north. The old road had fallen dormant for many years until construction of the trail brought it back to public use.

A proposed extension to the Windsor River Trail could incorporate it with other bike paths in the region. An effort in Hartford to create a multi-use trail along the Connecticut River north of Riverside Park (Chapter 17) could potentially connect this trail as well as the Capt. John Bissell Greenway (Chapter 20).

TRAIL POLICIES:

The Windsor River Trail is open to bicycling, in-line skating, walking, and running. Bicyclists and in-line skaters are asked to warn others when approaching from behind to avoid startling people. Travel at a safe speed and be especially cautious in the presence of small children since their movements can be unpredictable.

Horseback riding and motorized uses are prohibited. Pets must be leashed and pet wastes removed. Help keep the area litter-free by carrying out at least as much as you carry in. The area is open only during daylight hours.

ORIENTATION:

The Windsor River Trail forms a loop which is bounded by the center of town on one side and by the Farmington River on the other. Two spurs connect the loop to surrounding parks and parking lots, and each trail intersection is marked with wooden signs which point to the various destinations on the accompanying map. The trail does not intersect any roads. Given the area's small scale, it is difficult to be lost for long.

The trail's surface measures eight feet wide and has borders of mowed grass on each side. Its low-lying location along the banks of the Farmington River is subject to periodic river flooding so it could be impassible in times of especially wet weather.

TRAIL DESCRIPTION:

Starting from the trailhead parking lot on **Palisado Ave. (Rte. 159)** and following the loop in the clockwise direction, fork left on the paved pathway. Heading east, it descends a faint slope while winding through the tall trees of a mature forest. The trail and its manicured borders of grass curve through the woods purposefully, encouraging cyclists and skaters to travel slowly and appreciate the natural scenery. It eventually flattens and reaches a T-intersection beside the **Farmington River** after 0.2 miles.

Turning left and heading north at this intersection, the trail runs for a quarter-mile to **Pleasant St. Park**. It winds through more tall trees as it heads upstream along the Farmington and crosses a bridge over tributary **Mill Brook** along the way. The trail's pavement ends near Palisado Ave. but an unpaved trail loops under the bridge which carries the road over the river to reach the park on the other side. The park has a landscaped walkway overlooking the

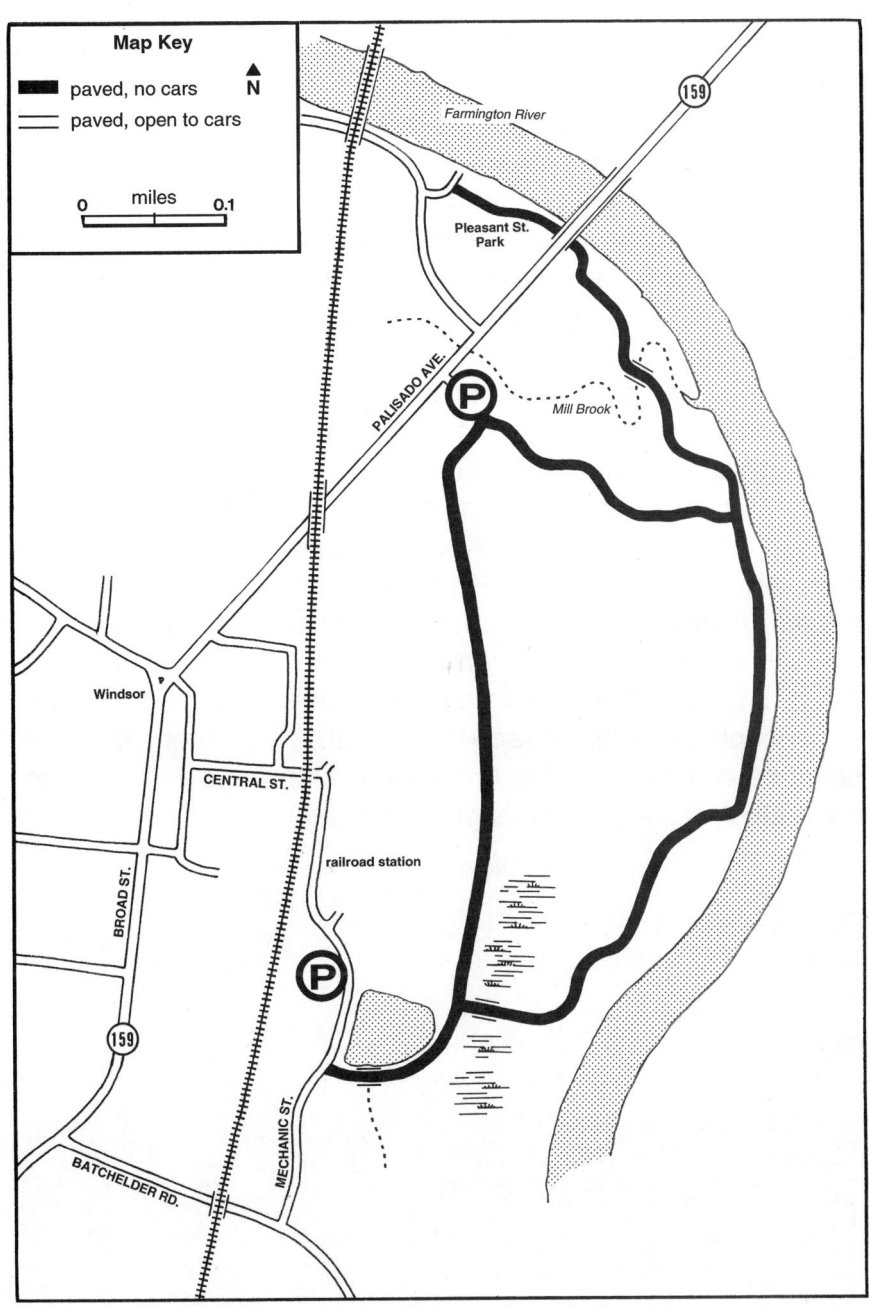

Map Key

▲ N

paved, no cars

paved, open to cars

miles

0   0.1

Farmington River

159

Pleasant St.
Park

PALISADO AVE.

Mill Brook

P

Windsor

CENTRAL ST.

railroad station

BROAD ST.

P

159

MECHANIC ST.

BATCHELDER RD.

river and a boat launch which is a focal point for local fishermen.

Turning south and continuing the main loop in the clockwise direction, the trail follows the Farmington River downstream. Forest foliage blocks the view of the river for much of the way but clearings exist and benches await at a few choice locations inviting visitors to stop and enjoy the tranquil scenery. As the river flows steadily toward its confluence with the Connecticut just a half-mile away, stately trees draped with a variety of vines tower overhead and provide complete shade for the forest floor.

The trail eventually turns westward and emerges from the woods at the edge of a wetland where an arched pedestrian/bicycle bridge carries the trail across a long span. On the other side, a second spur trail intersects on the left and circles a small pond, crosses a wooden bridge over an outlet brook, and ends at **Mechanic St.** near a public parking lot and the downtown business area.

Turning right and completing the last leg of the loop, the trail follows the colonial era road bed known as Rowland Lane back to the trailhead parking lot. Straighter than other sections of the loop, this 0.4-mile stretch passes behind the town DPW facility at the edge of the park.

DRIVING DIRECTIONS:

From I-91 take Exit 38 and follow Rte. 75 south for 2 miles to Windsor Center. Turn left (north) at the traffic signal on Rte. 159 north and drive for a quarter-mile to the parking lot on the right, just before a bridge over the Farmington River.

TOILET FACILITIES:

None on site

BIKE SHOPS:

Bicycle South Windsor, 978 Sullivan Ave., South Windsor,
(860) 644-0023

Bloomfield Bicycle, 5 Seneca Rd., Bloomfield, (860) 242-9884

Cyclist's Haven, 1077 Palisado Ave., Windsor, (860) 683-1616

Heinz's Ski & Bike, 4 Prospect Hill Rd., E. Windsor, (860) 292-6101

19
Windsor Locks Canal Towpath
Suffield - Windsor Locks

length: 4.4 miles
surface: pavement
terrain: flat
note: closed annually from mid-Nov. until early Apr.

The Windsor Locks Canal was once a valuable passageway for boats plying the Connecticut River and its towpath now enables cyclists, in-line skaters, walkers, and other self-propelled visitors to travel the same distance. The trail's isolated location along the river combines great natural scenery with an interesting relic of history.

BACKGROUND:

The Windsor Locks Canal was built by hand between 1827 and 1829. Over 400 Irish immigrants dug the five-and-a-half-mile channel using shovels and wheel barrows, excavating dirt and rock along a slope beside the river and piling it to form the banking that would become the towpath. The canal's depth was 4 and a half feet and its width was 80 feet, wide enough to accommodate steamboats. Three locks were built to bridge the 30-foot elevation change in the river and an aqueduct, still functioning, carries the canal above Stony Brook, a tributary stream. Horses pulled the boat traffic through the canal using the towpath.

The canal enabled boats to avoid Enfield Falls, a series of rapids which had marked the northernmost point on the river navigable by sea-going vessels. Its creation enhanced trade between the seacoast and inland areas including Vermont and Canada and served local industry until 1845, when the railroad arrived. It then continued functioning as a power source for nearby mills. Today, portions of the canal and towpath are owned and managed cooperatively by Northeast Utilities, the state of Connecticut, the Nature Conservancy, and the Dexter Corporation.

RULES OF THE TRAIL:

The Windsor Locks Canal Towpath is closed to all uses from mid-November until early April each year in order to protect the nesting habitat for endangered birds of prey. Chainlink gates are locked at each endpoint to prevent entry during this period.

During the remainder of the year, signs welcome pedestrians and bicyclists but warn visitors to "Pass at your own risk." When approaching others from behind, give a friendly greeting to avoid startling them. The area is open only during daylight hours.

ORIENTATION:

The towpath's paved surface measures 10 feet in width. A strip of mowed grass borders both sides but dense underbrush overhangs at many points, narrowing the perceived space of the trail and blocking some of the views. In other places, steep, unprotected bankings drop beside the trail and are a potential hazard for inattentive cyclists and small children.

The trail crosses no roads along its 4.4-mile length and is a completely car-free route. Visitors should note that, since water confines it on both sides, the trail is accessible only at the two ends and cannot be entered or exited from any point in between. Mileage is painted on the pavement at half-mile increments starting at the northern end, the most popular trailhead.

TRAIL DESCRIPTION:

Starting at the northern terminus at the end of **Canal Rd.** in Suffield, follow the trail across a bridge over the beginning of the **Windsor Locks Canal**. Chainlink fencing lines the bridge and an open vantage point allows an excellent view over the river, the rapids known as **Enfield Falls**, and the head of the canal.

The painted mileage markers begin at this point. Heading south, the towpath travels along the crest of a banking created when the canal was dug and follows a fairly

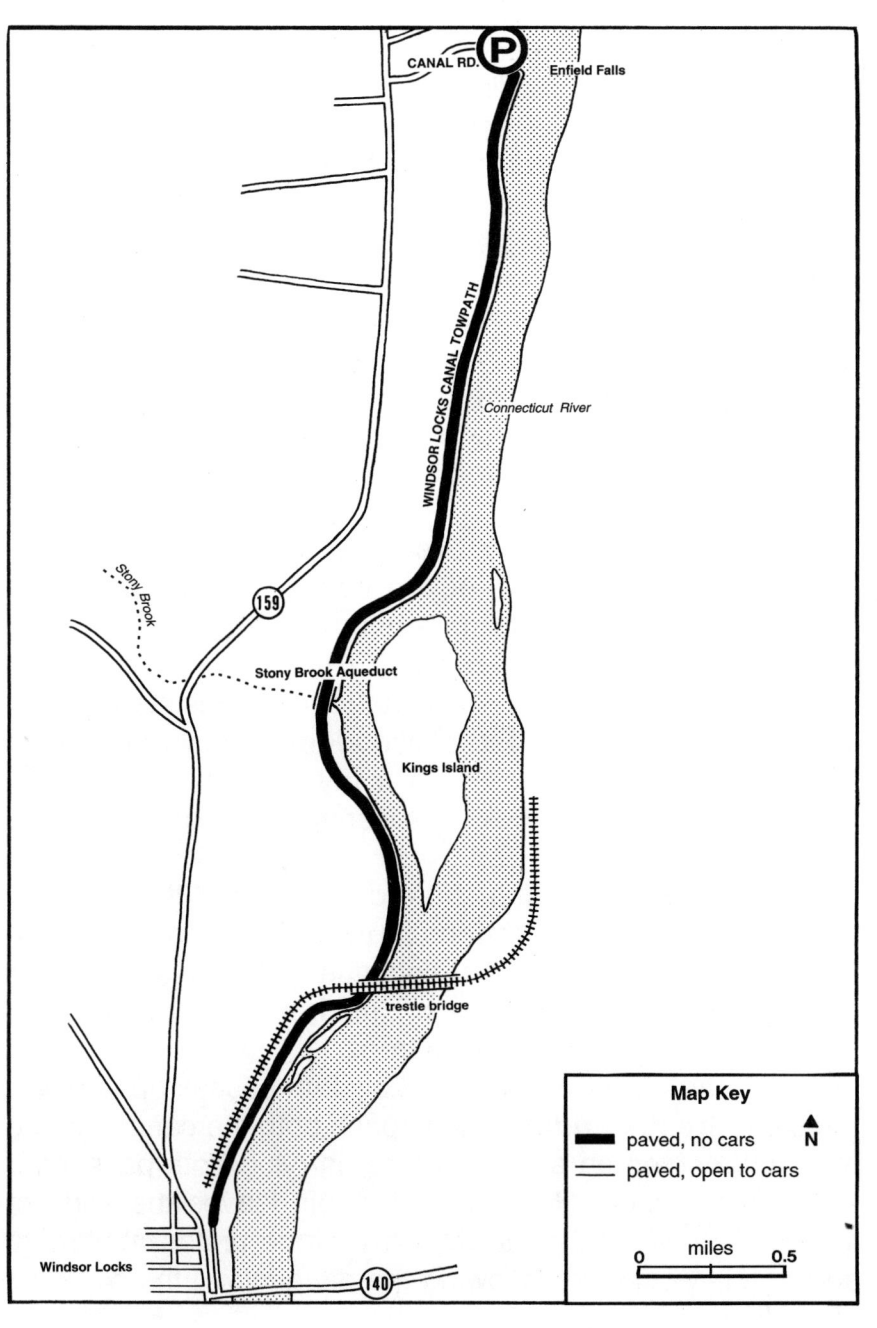

CANAL RD.
Enfield Falls

WINDSOR LOCKS CANAL TOWPATH

Connecticut River

Stony Brook

159

Stony Brook Aqueduct

Kings Island

trestle bridge

Windsor Locks

140

Map Key

N

▬▬▬ paved, no cars

═══ paved, open to cars

miles

0   0.5

straight line beside the river for the first 1.8 miles. Water in the canal borders the right side of the trail and the much larger flow of the Connecticut River is visible through trees on the left. A steep banking drops from the trail's pavement to the river's edge and deserves appropriate caution since no protective fencing exists for trail travelers.

Less than a mile from the parking lot, the terrain beside the trail steepens and the canal hugs the base of a high slope. Carved from the hillside in a massive effort, the canal's even, level channel is easily appreciated while rolling along this section of the towpath.

The trail arcs to the right after 1.8 miles where the Connecticut splits at **Kings Island**, and it continues for 1.3 miles along a narrower stretch of river which loops past the west side of the island.

Look for the **Stony Brook Aqueduct** just ahead at the 2.3-mile mark. One of the canal's most impressive features, the aqueduct forms a bridge for the water to pass six feet above **Stony Brook**, a tributary stream which crosses perpendicularly. The aqueduct consists of huge stone supports and a bed of wooden beams which have recently been reinforced with a layer of concrete. The towpath crosses the brook on a separate bridge beside the aqueduct.

The trail leaves the shore of the river at this point for the next half-mile, then returns to the edge of another steep banking above the water and continues past the southern tip of Kings Island. Glimpses of the full width of the river appear through windows in the trees.

At the 3.3-mile mark, the towpath passes underneath a railroad **trestle bridge** which spans both the canal and the river and serves an active rail line carrying both passenger and freight trains. Here the trail again leaves the edge of the river, turns hard right around a stone bridge abuttment and heads westward, following the canal along the contours of the land.

The last mile of trail turns back to the south and

returns to the sights and sounds of civilization. The river, towpath, canal, and railroad run shoulder-to-shoulder along the trail's last stretch to **Windsor Locks** with a wall of dense brush blocking most views. The trail ends at a small parking lot beside a mill complex off **Rte. 140**.

DRIVING DIRECTIONS:
From I-91, take Exit 47W and follow Rte. 190 west for 1.3 miles. Turn left at a traffic signal on Rte. 159 south and continue for a short distance, then take the first left on Canal Rd. Park in the lot at the end.

TOILET FACILITIES:
Toilets are not provided.

BIKE SHOPS:
Cyclist's Haven, 1077 Palisado Ave., Windsor, (860) 683-1616
Enfield Bicycle Shop, 630 Enfield St., Enfield, (860) 745-4006
Heinz's Ski & Bike, 4 Prospect Hill Rd., E. Windsor, (860) 292-6101
State Line Cycles, 270 Enfield St., Enfield, (860) 253-0221

ADDITIONAL INFORMATION:
Connecticut Dept. of Environmental Protection, 79 Elm St., Hartford, CT 06106-5127, Tel. (860) 424-3200
web: http://dep.state.ct.us

20
Capt. John Bissell Greenway
East Hartford - Windsor

length: 7.4 miles (includes 3-mile segment on roads)
surface: pavement
terrain: moderate hills

In heroic style, the Capt. John Bissell Greenway slips through the ramps and overpasses of three interstate highways and spans the Connecticut River to provide safe passage for bicycle commuters and other self-propelled travelers. If you don't mind contending with highway noise at several points, following an on-road bike route for part of the way, and facing a few hills, it is easy to appreciate what this path delivers.

BACKGROUND:
The greenway is named for Capt. John Bissell (1591-1677) who founded Windsor. It was created in conjunction with the construction of I-291 and opened in 1996.

The Capt. John Bissell Greenway is free of the high traffic levels found at some of the state's other bike paths but the presence of nearby automobile traffic curtails any feelings of solitude. The trail intersects the Charter Oak Greenway (Chapter 21) and is part of a growing network of bicycle trails east of Hartford.

RULES OF THE TRAIL:
Cyclists should keep to the right side, pass on the left, and warn others before passing them to avoid any surprises. The trail encounters several hills and corners with limited visibility so ride at a safe speed and be ready to meet others coming in the opposite direction.

ORIENTATION:
The Capt. John Bissell Greenway is aligned primarily in the east-west direction and its midsection is a 2.9-mile marked bicycle route on local roads. The eastern

segment of the bike path measures 3.1 miles long, intersects the Charter Oak Greenway (Chapter 21), and holds the curviest, hilliest conditions and the most separation from surrounding highways. The western end of the bike path measures 1.4 miles long, follows the side of a highway, and ends at Windsor Meadows State Park.

Wickham Park (seasonal) is the best starting point for the greenway. A small entrance fee is charged and the park is open daily from 9:30 AM until dusk from early April through late October. From the entrance, the greenway extends southward for 1.1 miles to the Charter Oak Greenway in East Hartford and northward for 6.3 miles to Windsor.

The bike path varies between 10 and 14 feet wide and is bordered by protective fencing where necessary. Signs point to destinations at points along the way and crosswalks exist where the bike path meets roads. The bike route portion of the greenway is clearly marked along local roads by green signs at the major intersections.

TRAIL DESCRIPTION:

Wickham Park is the recommended starting point. The 250-acre property was once the home of Clarence H. Wickham, a local industrialist who desired that it become a parkland for all to enjoy. Managed by a private organization, the park offers manicured grounds, picnic areas, fields, gardens, and a great view over the Hartford area.

Leaving the Wickham Park entrance gate, turn left to find the bike path. To follow it southward, cross **Rte. 44** and continue along the path as it parallels the roadway, then veers to the right near a highway off-ramp. It follows the broad turns of this roadway for most of the first half-mile but earthen embankments and foliage buffer the trail from the sight of traffic for most of the way. Descending gradually, it eventually merges with the edge of the roadway, crosses a bridge over the **Hockanum River**, and then turns 270 degrees in a loop that redirects the path under the highway bridge beside the river. Climbing a strenuous slope on the

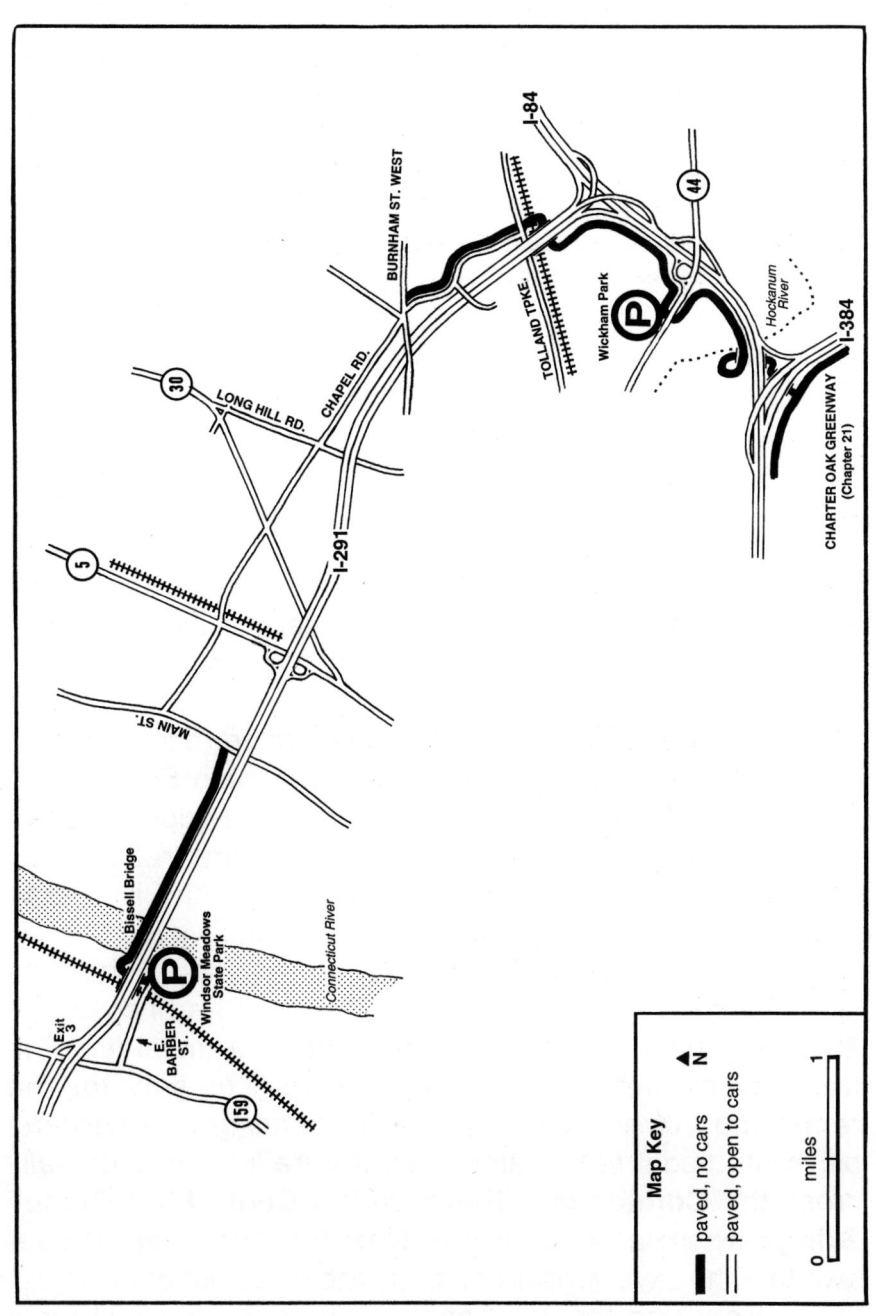

Map Key

▲N

▬▬ paved, no cars

═══ paved, open to cars

0 —— miles —— 1

other side, the path joins a barrier beside **I-84** for a short distance and then turns south, passes under a ramp for **I-384**, and ends at the **Charter Oak Greenway** (Chapter 21).

Heading north from Wickham Park, the trail follows a wooden fence beside Rte. 44 for a tenth of a mile, then turns left and begins a half-mile climb which starts beside a highway off-ramp and later enters its own space bound by earthen bankings on both sides. Topping this hill, the path descends for a short distance to the side of **I-291** where protective fencing leads it over mostly flat ground.

Near the 1-mile mark, the path turns and passes underneath a bridge carrying the highway over a set of railroad tracks and the **Tolland Tpke.** A short distance beyond, the path crosses the tracks and the turnpike at a crosswalk and continues beside **Chapel Rd.** through an industrial park. The paved surface of the bike path is badly cracked along this portion of the ride. After following Chapel Rd. for about a mile the path ends near the intersection of **Burnham St. West** near the South Windsor town line, 2 miles from Wickham Park.

A marked bike route continues west from this point on Chapel Rd. for an additional 2.5 miles to **Main St.**, where it turns left and runs for another 0.4 miles. Although the route crosses a few busy roads, it holds moderate traffic levels and remains in mostly residential areas. Green Bike Route signs bearing the image of a bicycle mark the way.

Look for the separated path to resume on the right side just before Main St. passes underneath a bridge for I-291. The path ascends gradually beside a metal fence to the side of the highway and follows it closely for the remaining 1.4 miles. Protected by fencing and barriers, bicyclists pedal safely alongside the traffic and eventually cross the **Connecticut River** on the **Capt. John Bissell Bridge** where a great view of New England's largest river awaits. The skyline of Hartford is visible downstream.

Reaching the west bank of the river, the trail turns and descends beneath the highway at another set of railroad tracks and ends at **Windsor Meadows State Park**, 6.3 miles from Wickham Park. Windsor Meadows State Park is a boat launching site and its large parking lot serves as an alternate trailhead for the bike path.

DRIVING DIRECTIONS:

To reach Wickham Park (seasonal) from I-84 take Exit 60 and follow Rte. 44 west. Look for the park entrance immediately ahead on the right.

To reach Windsor Meadows State Park from I-91 northbound take Exit 34 and follow signs to Rte. 159. Turn right on Rte. 159 north and drive for 0.7 miles, then turn right on E. Barber St. and continue to the end.

From I-91 southbound, take Exit 35B and follow Rte. 218 east for a half-mile. Turn right on Rte. 159 south and drive for a third of a mile, then turn left on E. Barber St. Park at the end.

From I-291 westbound, take Exit 3 and follow signs to Rte. 159 south. After a third of a mile on Rte. 159 south, turn left on E. Barber St. and park at the end.

TOILET FACILITIES:

Toilets are available in season at Wickham Park and at Windsor Meadows State Park.

BIKE SHOPS:

Bicycle South Windsor, 978 Sullivan Ave., South Windsor,
    (860) 644-0023
Bike Shop, 681 Main St., Manchester, (860) 429-4532
Bloomfield Bicycle, 5 Seneca Rd., Bloomfield, (860) 242-9884
Cyclist's Haven, 1077 Palisado Ave., Windsor, (860) 683-1616
E-Trans, 1026 Main St., East Hartford, (860) 289-8485
Farr's, 2 Main St., Manchester, (860) 643-7111
Manchester Cycles, 178 W. Middle Tpke., Manchester,
    (860) 649-2098
Ski & Bike Market, 432 Buckland Hills Dr., Manchester,
    (860) 644-6200
Vernon Cycle, 352 Hartford Tpke., Vernon, (860) 872-7740

ADDITIONAL INFORMATION:

Connecticut Dept. of Environmental Protection, 79 Elm St., Hartford, CT 06106-5127, Tel. (860) 424-3200
web: http://dep.state.ct.us

Wickham Park, 1329 West Middle Tpke., Manchester, CT 06040, Tel. (860) 528-0856

21
Charter Oak Greenway
East Hartford-Manchester

length: 6.3 miles
surface: paved
terrain: hilly

Recently extended, Manchester's greenway is a rolling, turning ribbon of asphalt which shadows an interstate highway in an enjoyable, landscaped setting. It is a mostly off-road route but follows local roads at a few points.

BACKGROUND:

The Charter Oak Greenway was conceived in 1972 during the planning stages for the construction of Interstate 384. Early visionaries dreamed of a safe passageway beside the highway to enable walkers, runners, bicyclists, and other human-powered travelers to reach their destinations and in 1994 it became a reality. The Federal Highway Administration provided the bulk of the funding for the project and the state contributed the remainder.

The greenway is named for one of the state's most famous hiding places. In 1687 when the King's agents arrived in Hartford with armed force demanding to take the Charter from the General Court of Connecticut, daring colonials hid the document inside an old oak tree nearby. The Charter Oak no longer stands but it remains one of Connecticut's most enduring symbols of liberty.

The greenway intersects the Capt. John Bissell Greenway (Chapter 20) which continues westward to Windsor. It also holds the possibility of being extended eastward to Bolton and forms a link in the planned 500-mile East Coast Greenway.

RULES OF THE TRAIL:

The bike path encounters steep slopes and blind corners as it winds through a complex landscape of roads, bridges, and woodlands. Some of the hills are marked by signs and many of the sharp turns have a yellow dividing line, but few other warnings exist so bicyclists should keep to the right side, ride at a safe speed, and be ready to yield to others on the path. When crossing roads, stop before entering the roadway and assume that drivers do not see you.

ORIENTATION:

The Charter Oak Greenway stretches from Gardner St. in Manchester to Forbes St. in East Hartford alongside I-384 and I-84, although it diverges at several points and crosses the highway at three locations using local roads. Bike Route signs mark the intersections along the three on-road sections of the greenway and crosswalks are in place at road crossings.

The paved surface is 10 feet wide with a border of mowed grass on each side. Protective fencing shields the trail and prevents trail users from entering the highway.

TRAIL DESCRIPTION:

Charter Oak Park, located near the eastern end of the greenway, provides the best starting point for the trail and offers a large parking lot, toilet facilities (in season), and direct access to the greenway.

Heading east (left) on the trail from the parking lot, the newest section of the Charter Oak Greenway extends for about 0.6 miles. It leaves the open area of the ball fields, intersects a side trail which runs underneath the highway to additional playing fields, and continues into a woodsy area of tall trees beside Porter Brook and the highway. After passing a few apartment buildings, the trail approaches the **Gardner St.** overpass where it bends to the left and soon ends at West Gardner St.

Heading west (right) on the trail from the parking lot, the pathway dips beneath off- and on-ramps for I-384, circles a playing field, and emerges at the intersection of **Charter Oak St.** and **Main St.** Turn hard left at this point and ride south along Main St. (crossing over I-384) and look

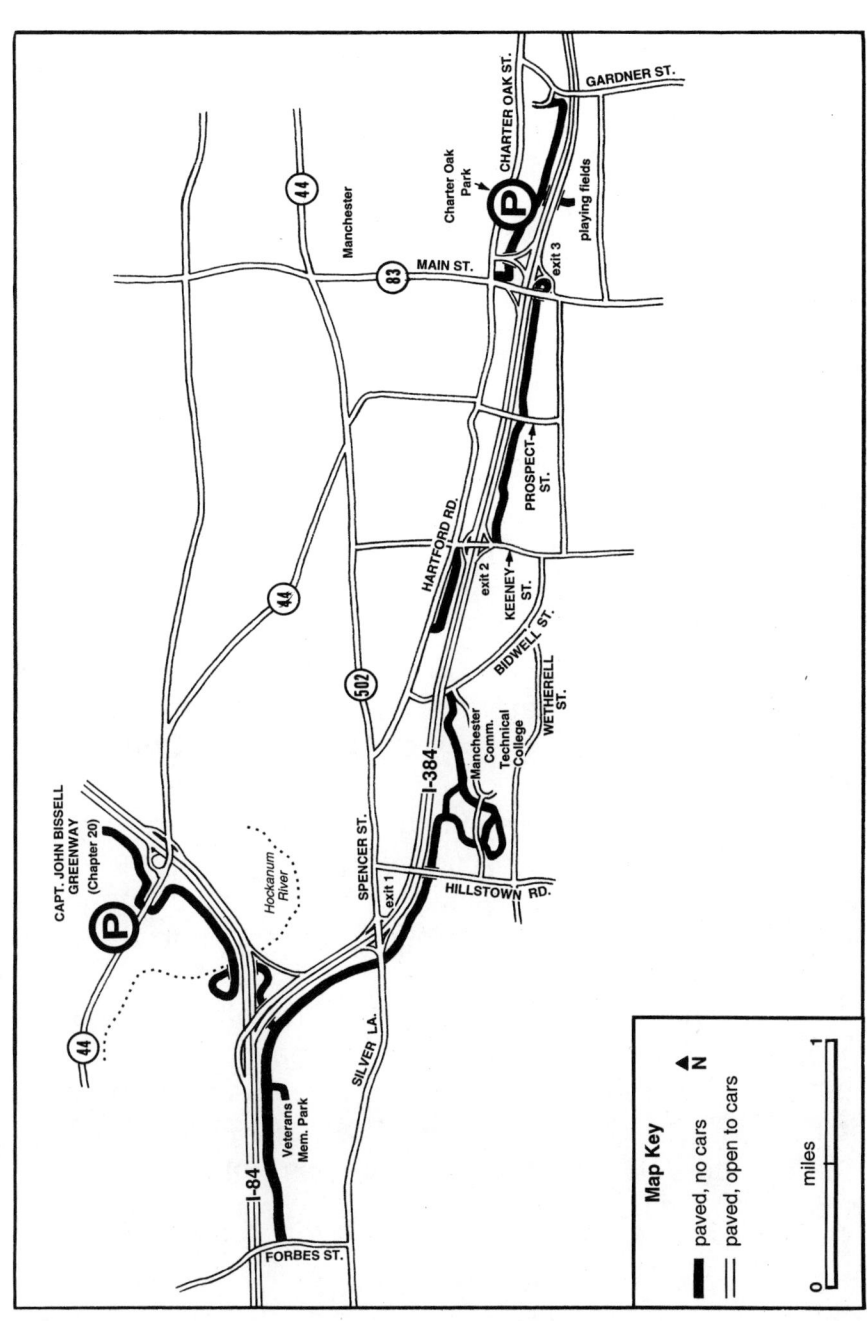

for a Bike Route sign marking the greenway on the left side before an off-ramp at Exit 3.

The bike path turns on a downslope beside the exit ramp and eventually passes underneath Main St. It follows the edge of the highway for a third of a mile, climbs a hill to cross **Prospect St.**, descends back to side of the freeway, then climbs to **Keeney St.** where another on-road segment begins 1.8 miles from Charter Oak Park. Following more Bike Route signs, riders turn right on Keeney and cross back to the north side of the interstate where the separated bike path resumes on the left before **Hartford Rd.**

The next half-mile of trail parallels Hartford Rd. in a landscaped strip of greenspace. At the end, the trail emerges on Hartford Rd. at the beginning of the last, and longest, on-road segment of the greenway. Turn left on Hartford Rd. and ride for a third of a mile, turn left on **Bidwell St.**, cross underneath the highway, and look for the bike path on the right.

It begins with a strenuous uphill which returns riders to the side of the interstate, then turns and descends through woods to the campus of **Manchester Community Tech. College**. Curving between ballfields, parking lots, and quiet woodlands on a mile-long detour from the highway, the paved pathway enjoys some of its most peaceful surroundings along this distance. A few intersecting paths link the campus and provide alternative loops to the main greenway route.

The greenway returns to the side of I-384 about 4 miles from Charter Oak Park. After passing underneath **Hillstown Rd.** the bike path veers uphill beside an on-ramp at Exit 1, crosses **Silver La./Spencer St.** at the East Hartford border, and descends in a straight line along a wooden sound barrier built beside the highway.

A half-mile of uphill pedaling ensues as the greenway arcs to the left and joins the side of I-84. Halfway up the slope it intersects the end of the **Capt. John Bissell Greenway** (Chapter 20), 5.2 miles from the parking lot at

Charter Oak Park. At the top of the hill it intersects a short, steep spur linking **Veterans Memorial Park** and also enjoys a view of the Hartford skyline before tilting downward on a long slope. The final 0.7 miles to **Forbes St.** in East Hartford benefits from a greater separation from the highway as well as more wooden sound barriers to block traffic noise.

DRIVING DIRECTIONS:

From I-384 eastbound take Exit 3. Turn right off the ramp and follow Main St. north to the first traffic signal. Turn right on Charter Oak St. and continue to the next traffic signal, then turn right at the entrance to Charter Oak Park.

From I-384 westbound, take Exit 3. Turn right off the ramp on Charter Oak St., continue to the next traffic signal, then turn right at the the entrance to Charter Oak Park.

TOILET FACILITIES:

Toilets are located at Charter Oak Park.

BIKE SHOPS:

Bicycle South Windsor, 978 Sullivan Ave., South Windsor, (860) 644-0023

Bicycles East, 2333 Main St., Glastonbury, (860) 659-0114

Bike Shop, 681 Main St., Manchester, (860) 429-4532

E-Trans, 1026 Main St., East Hartford, (860) 289-8485

Farr's, 2 Main St., Manchester, (860) 643-7111

Manchester Cycles, 178 W. Middle Tpke., Manchester, (860) 649-2098

Pig Iron Bicycle Works, 38 Addison Rd., Glastonbury, (860) 659-8808

Ski & Bike Market, 432 Buckland Hills Dr., Manchester, (860) 644-6200

Vernon Cycle, 352 Hartford Tpke., Vernon, (860) 872-7740

Wethersfield Bicycle, 212 Church St., Wethersfield, (860) 563-3000

ADDITIONAL INFORMATION:

Manchester Parks & Recreation Dept., P.O. Box 191, Manchester, CT 06045-0191, Tel. (860) 647-3084

22
Hammonassett Beach State Park
Madison

length: 2 miles
surface: mostly stone dust, partly old pavement
terrain: flat

Hammonasset's main attraction is a 2-mile ocean beach but its bike path has been motivating a growing number of visitors to walk, run, and ride through the cool sea breezes and beautiful coastal scenery. Given its exposed location, this path is not recommended during especially windy weather.

BACKGROUND:

Hammonassett, a Native American name which means "where we dig holes in the ground," was settled in the late 1630's and supported a small agricultural and fishing community for a few hundred years. Settlers processed fish for fertilizer and oil, harvested salt hay from the marshes, and grew potatoes and wheat in the fields. In the late 1890's a local arms manufacturer used the peninsula as a rifle range.

Hammonassett Beach State Park was established in 1919 when the first parcels of land were acquired by the state. The park officially opened in July, 1920 and quickly became a popular attraction for growing numbers of summer vacationers from distant places who arrived by car and camped beside the shore. Colonies of summer cottages sprouted near the park during this period. Today, Hammonassett's campground holds a huge capacity and its 2-mile beach draws thousands of visitors on peak days, making it one of Connecticut's most popular parks.

RULES OF THE TRAIL:

Cyclists should plan on slow speeds when riding Hammonasset's bike path since it measures only 8-10 feet wide in places and is busy with walkers on summer weekends. Be especially careful where beach access paths intersect the bike path and in the presence of children. Park staff remind pedalers to stay on the path at all times to avoid damaging the fragile environment of the surrounding dunes and marshes. Bikes are not allowed on the wooden boardwalks along the beaches.

A parking fee is charged at the entrance gate during the summer season. Alcohol is not permitted at the park, dogs are not allowed on the beach, and the park closes at sunset each day.

ORIENTATION:

Small, brown signs bearing the image of a bicycle are the only markings for the path but visitors will find that its short length, open scenery, and numerous landmarks make it easy to navigate. Five parking lots (each with toilet facilities open during the summer season) stationed along the path access both the beach and the bike path.

The main portion of the bike path parallels the shoreline for 1.3 miles between West Beach and Meigs Point with a firm surface of stone dust, and follows the park's access road for part of the way. A secondary portion of trail ventures northward from the Meigs Point area to Willards Island with a surface of old pavement.

TRAIL DESCRIPTIONS:

Begin at **West Beach**, Hammonasset's largest parking area. Facing the water, the bike path runs to the right for only a tenth of a mile before ending at a picnic pavilion but runs to the left for a mile and a quarter to the Meigs Point parking lots.

Following the path southward along the shoreline, cyclists pedal beside dunes which separate the beach area with a green swathe of tall grasses, red cedars, and beach roses. A mowed field occupies the other side of the trail with picnic tables and plenty of room to play. After a third of a mile, the bike path arcs past the **Central Pavilion** where toilets and a deck with more tables are housed in a modern,

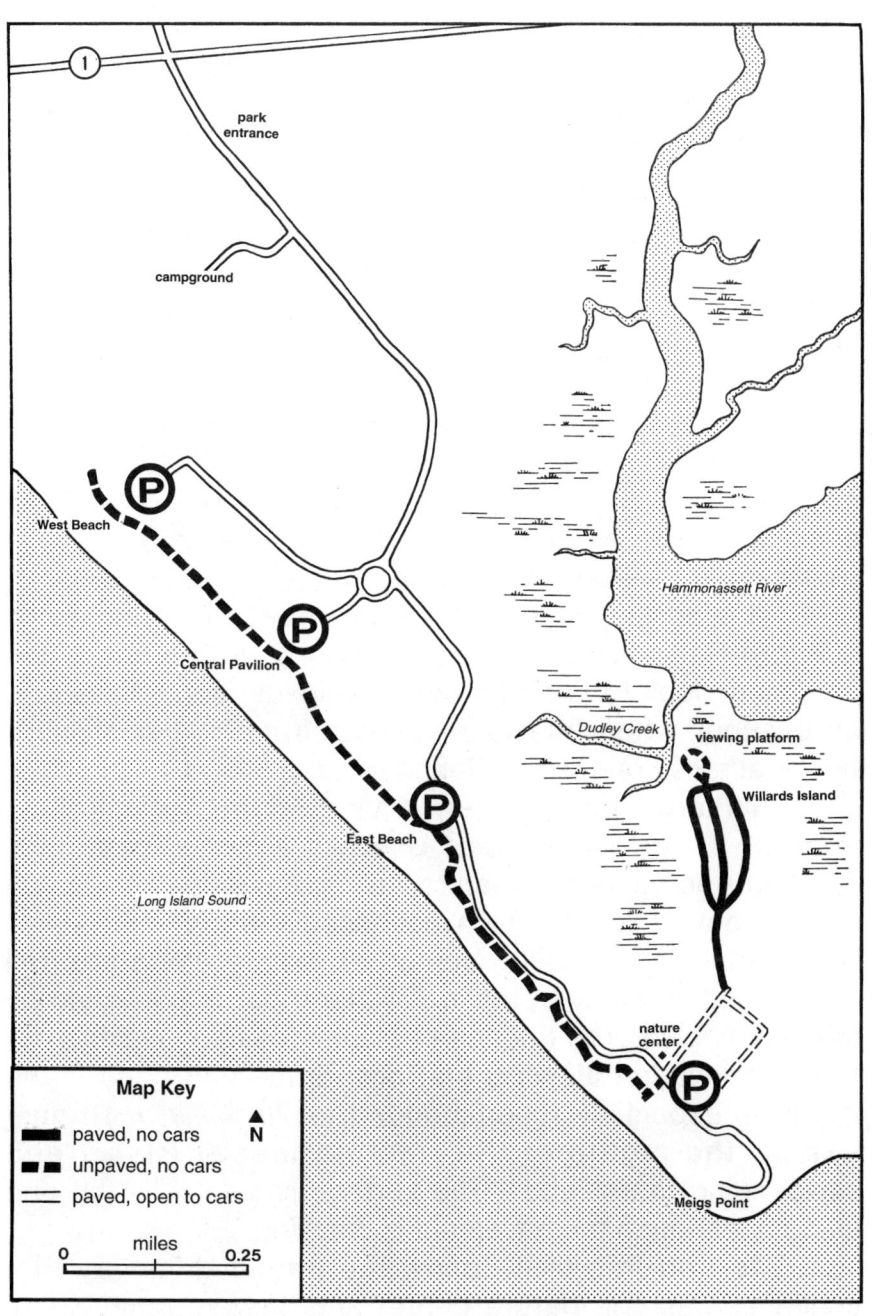

Map Key

▲N

▬▬ paved, no cars

▬ ▬ unpaved, no cars

══ paved, open to cars

0   miles   0.25

1

park entrance

campground

West Beach

Central Pavilion

East Beach

Long Island Sound

Hammonassett River

Dudley Creek

viewing platform

Willards Island

nature center

Meigs Point

concrete structure.

The trail returns to natural surroundings for most of the next third of a mile to the **East Beach** parking lot and beach house where a long, flat-roofed structure offers more facilities. Crossing a section of the paved parking lot at this point, the path slips through a small grove of cedars, turns toward the shoreline, then joins a paved surface for a short distance. At the 0.8-mile mark, it reaches the side of the park's access road and turns right on an unpaved surface which follows the edge of the roadway for 0.2 miles. The beach and its crashing waves lie closeby but dunes block the view.

Next, the path separates from the road for a short distance and then returns to its side for another tenth of a mile before turning into a last area of dunes and grasses. It ends near the **Meigs Point** parking lot and beach house where more facilities await.

It is possible to continue on the road for an additional quarter-mile to the end of the peninsula. At the end of the pavement, look for a hiking path that leads up a small hill to an overlook where the view spreads from Hammonasset's beach across Long Island Sound to Long Island.

Willards Island offers a worthwhile, 0.8-mile loop from the Meigs Point area. Used as a campground until 1972, this acreage has been reclaimed by dense foliage and the old paved roads which accessed the campsites now serve as a nature trail. Numbered points along the trail correspond to an interpretive brochure that is published by the volunteer group, Friends of Hammonasset Beach State Park. A wooden **viewing platform** at the north end of the island is especially recommended for its view of **Dudley Creek**, the mouth of the **Hammonasset River**, and surrounding marshland. The surface is generally flat and smooth, although the pavement is cracking.

To find this trail, follow the paved driveway that continues past the **nature center** and the large parking lot beside a field. The road ends at a gate at the northern edge of a mowed field, where the trail begins.

DRIVING DIRECTIONS:
From I-95 take Exit 62 and drive south on the Hammonasset Connector for 1.3 miles to a traffic signal at Rte. 1. Continue straight through the intersection to the park's entrance gate. Each of the major parking areas is clearly marked with signs along the main access road.

TOILET FACILITIES:
Toilets are available at the beach parking lots.

BIKE SHOPS:
Cycle & Sport, 17 E. Main St., Clinton, (860) 669-5228
Cycles of Madison, 698 Boston Post Rd., Madison, (203) 245-8735

ADDITIONAL INFORMATION:
Hammonasset Beach State Park, Box 271, Madison, CT 06443, Tel. (203) 245-2785
Campground: (203) 245-1817

23
Hop River State Park Trail
Manchester - Columbia

length: 20 miles, plus a 3.4-mile spur to Rockville
surface: varies between stone dust, crushed stone, dirt
terrain: gradual slopes

One of Connecticut's longest rail-trails, the Hop River connects the Manchester and Willimantic areas with a woodsy route through Bolton Notch. Conditions vary from smooth and tidy to rough and overgrown.

BACKGROUND:
The Hop River State Park Trail follows the route of the former Hartford, Providence, and Fishkill Railroad which was constructed in 1854. For about 100 years, it provided a direct connection between the Connecticut and Rhode Island state capitols as well as a valuable link to the outside world for the many small towns along the route.

The state's Dept. of Transportation acquired the line after bankruptcy ended the operation, then transferred it to the Dept. of Environmental Protection in 1987 for recreational use. Vernon, with help of the National Guard, began developing its portions in 1995. Look for future improvements along the less-developed sections since this trail is an important part of the East Coast Greenway, a proposed bike trail between Maine and Florida.

RULES OF THE TRAIL:
Bicyclists should plan to share the trail with walkers, runners, horseback riders, and others. Keep to the right, ride at a safe speed, and give a warning before passing others to avoid startling them. Use extra caution when approaching horses since they are easily frightened by bicycles, and ask for the rider's advice before passing.

Hunting occurs in areas surrounding the trail. During the period from mid-October to late December (the most popular time for hunting), riders are encouraged to wear blaze orange clothing except on Sundays, when hunting is prohibited by state law.

ORIENTATION:

This description covers 20 miles of the Hop River State Park Trail from Manchester to Vernon, Bolton, Andover, Columbia, Coventry and the Willimantic River. The 5.1-mile Vernon portion has the trail's best conditions with a smooth surface of stone dust, crosswalks at road intersections, benches, historical markers, and an official trailhead parking lot. Other sections remain untouched and a few spots suffer from rough and overgrown conditions.

Three bridges along the easternmost 6 miles of trail warrant extreme caution when crossing since they lack proper decking. Courageous trail users carefully walk across on the span's massive, iron supports but others will want to either turn back or detour on surrounding roads.

Given its superior condition and trailhead parking lot, the Vernon section is the recommended starting point. Bolton Notch also offers public parking but the adjoining trail surface is rough at a few points and its elevation (the trail's highest) makes it important for cyclists to save extra energy for the uphill return leg of their ride. Minimal space for parking exists at other trail/road intersections.

TRAIL DESCRIPTION:

Heading west from the **Church St.** trailhead in Vernon, the Hop River State Park Trail runs for 2.3 miles. The first 1.6 miles have smooth rolling on a stone dust surface with a slight downhill grade for much of the way but, at the border of Manchester, the trail's appearance changes. The remaining 0.7 miles to **Colonial Rd.** are not maintained and have a surface of hard-packed dirt which is made narrower in places by overgrowing weeds and branches.

Heading east from the Church St. trailhead, the Hop River State Park Trail extends for 17.6 miles to the Willimantic River although most cyclists will turn back at the 14.1-mile mark upon seeing the poor condition of the bridge over the Hop River. The trail leaves the parking lot at the site of the Vernon Depot and descends abruptly at the site of a missing bridge over Phoenix St.

Here a sign on the left marks the intersecting **Rockville Spur Rail-Trail**, a 3.4-mile route venturing north to the village of Rockville. This trail is mostly downhill for the first half and uphill for the second half and has a smooth surface of stone dust. It starts as a paved sidewalk along Warren Ave., then crosses the road and continues into the woods on a route which crosses over the Tankerhoosen River, passes underneath **I-84**, and intersects five other roads including busy **Rte. 30** at the 0.8-mile mark.

The Hop River Trail continues east from Phoenix St. past several residential neighborhoods and rises on a gradual slope which lasts for the next 4 miles to Bolton Notch. The trail follows the top of a long, earthen causeway as it crosses high above **Tunnel Rd.**, named for its one-lane passageway beneath the rail bed, about a mile from the parking lot. It then turns southward in a broad curve to the right and enters some of its best scenery, climbing at a more noticeable pace along the side of **Box Hill** with outcroppings of ledge looming above the trail on one side and the valley of Railroad Brook falling away on the other.

Near the 2-mile mark, a foot trail descends on the left to **Valley Falls Park** which is owned by the town of Vernon. At 3.4 miles the trail hits the Bolton town line where the stone dust surface degrades to a coarse combination of large-size crushed stone and hard-packed dirt, and the stream valley tightens to a narrow gap.

The **Bolton Notch** parking lot, which also serves a boat launch for nearby Bolton Notch Pond, appears at 4.4 miles on the right after a cut in the bedrock. The trail flattens and passes underneath the curved arch of the **Rte. 6/Rte. 44** bridge, then continues for almost a half-mile below ground level in another cut blasted into the top of the notch.

Descending gradually from this high point for most of its remaining distance, the Hop River State Park Trail turns

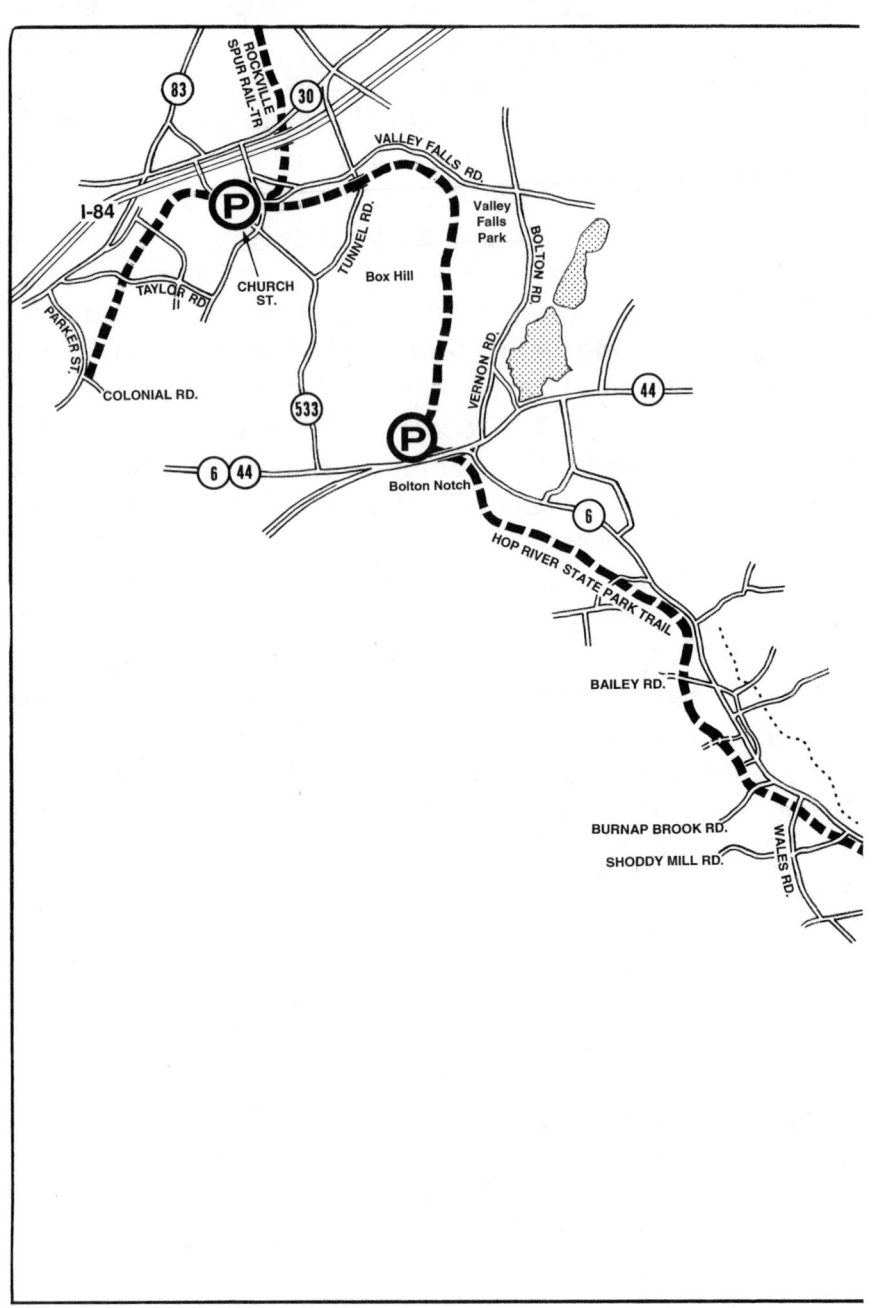

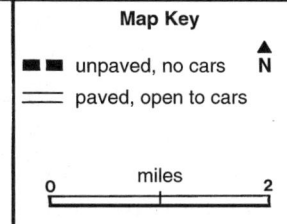

Map Key

■ ■ unpaved, no cars   ▲
              N
═══ paved, open to cars

0   miles   2

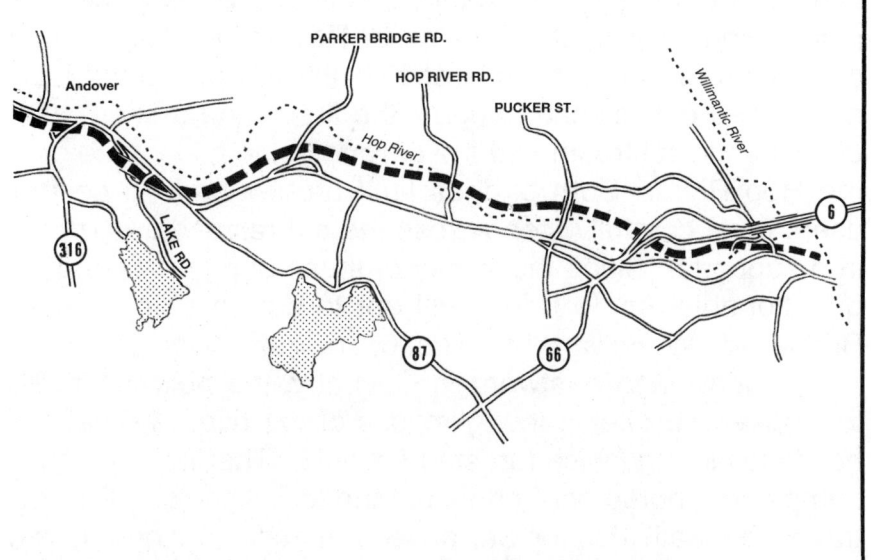

PARKER BRIDGE RD.

HOP RIVER RD.

PUCKER ST.

Andover

Hop River

Willimantic River

6

316

LAKE RD.

87

66

with the contours of a forested slope and shows few signs of civilization for the next 2.8 miles to **Bailey Rd.** in Andover. With the exception of a few rough spots, the surface remains smooth and firm. Less than a half-mile from Bailey Rd., cyclists should watch for a brief detour around a small railroad bridge which has lost its decking.

The trail crosses **Burnap Brook Rd.** near the 9-mile mark, then hits **Wales Rd.** and **Shoddy Mill Rd.** in the next 0.9 miles. Approaching the center of **Andover** at the 10-mile mark, it merges beside Rte. 6, passes just to the right of a large garage structure, and continues for a quarter-mile to the site of a missing bridge over **Rte. 316**. A barricade forces riders to stop and walk down the embankment to cross the road. To continue, follow the road marked Dead End to the left of the rail bed, then take the first right.

The rail bed's downhill slant becomes almost flat as the trail reaches **Lake Rd.** in another three quarters of a mile and passes through a long tunnel underneath Rte. 6 about 11.6 miles from the Vernon trailhead, or 7.2 miles from Bolton Notch. It crosses the Columbia town line at **Parker Bridge Rd.** and joins the banks of the **Hop River** at several points along the next 1.3 miles to **Hop River Rd.** Rough conditions return along this stretch and cyclists must walk across two old railroad bridges, the first being a short span across an inlet stream and the second being a long one over the Hop River. Both bridges lack proper decking so trail users must carefully step across the old railroad ties on the iron supports. Since the safety of these bridge crossings is questionable, some riders will opt to detour using Parker Bridge Rd., Woodward Rd., Rte. 6, and Hop River Rd.

Continuing eastward in Coventry, the next 1.1 miles to **Pucker St.** offer a few glimpses of the river and several hay fields in otherwise forested scenery. The trail surface is bumpy from horse hoof prints but the terrain is flat. The trail travels beneath Pucker St., passes through a sand pit, and crosses underneath two bridges carrying Rte. 6 about 16.1-miles from the Vernon trailhead.

The next 0.7 miles to Kings Rd. are smooth and clear but cyclists soon brake for another decrepit railroad bridge over the Hop River. Again, those willing can carefully walk across on the iron supports which hold the railroad ties. The trail returns to Columbia on the other side and lasts for another 0.8 miles to the **Willimantic River**, where the beaten path ends 17.6 miles from the Vernon trailhead.

DRIVING DIRECTIONS:

To reach the Vernon trailhead from I-84 eastbound, take Exit 64-65 and follow signs for Rte. 30 north. Turn right at the first traffic signal on Dobson Rd. (which becomes Washington St.), cross the highway, and take the second left on Church St. Parking is a third of a mile ahead on the left.

To reach the Vernon trailhead from I-84 westbound, take Exit 65 and follow Rte. 30 south. Turn left on Dobson Rd. (which becomes Washington St.), take the second left on Church St., and park a third of a mile ahead on the left.

To reach the Bolton Notch trailhead from I-384, drive to the eastern end of the expressway, fork left on Rte. 44 east, then take the first left at signs for Rte. 44 west (in order to reverse your direction). Continue on Rte. 44 west for less than a half-mile and turn right on a narrow road at a "boat launch" sign. Park at the bottom of the hill beside the trail.

TOILET FACILITIES:

Available (in season) at the Vernon trailhead.

BIKE SHOPS:

Bike Shop, 681 Main St., Manchester, (860) 429-4532
Bikes Plus, 30 Lafayette Sq., Rockville, (860) 872-6263
Cycle Escape, 50 Main St., Hebron, (860) 228-2453
Farr's, 2 Main St., Manchester, (860) 643-7111
Manchester Cycles, 178 W. Middle Tpke., Manchester,
    (860) 649-2098
Mountain City Cycle, 642 Tolland Stage Rd., Tolland, (860) 871-9559
Rainbow Cycle Sport, 385 Valley St., Willimantic, (860) 423-7182
Scott's Cyclery, 1171 Main St., Willimantic, (860) 423-8889
Ski & Bike Market, 432 Buckland Hills Dr., Manchester,
    (860) 644-6200
Vernon Cycle, 352 Hartford Tpke., Vernon, (860) 872-7740

ADDITIONAL INFORMATION:

Connecticut Dept. of Environmental Protection, 79 Elm St., Hartford, CT 06106-5127, Tel. (860) 424-3200,
web: http://dep.state.ct.us

24
Airline State Park Trail
E. Hampton - Hebron

length: 10.7 miles
surface: stone dust
terrain: gradual slopes

The Airline State Park Trail's long, slow turns and gentle slopes defy the surrounding terrain by blasting through its hillsides and spanning its valleys for an easy, scenic ride. This southern leg of the trail has been upgraded with new bridges and a smooth, firm surface.

BACKGROUND:

The trail follows the route of the Air Line Railroad, built in 1873 on an "air-line" course between New York and Boston. Since it bypassed Connecticut's capitol, construction of a direct route between the two cities faced political controversy as well as natural obstacles including a crossing of the Connecticut River and a rough topography. The Air Line's relatively hilly, curvey profile eventually restricted its success as trains began to carry heavier loads and opted for flatter routes. A flood in 1955 destroyed the railroad's bridge over the Quinebaug River in Putnam and it was never rebuilt.

The Connecticut Dept. of Environmental Protection (D.E.P.) proposed redeveloping the railbed as a linear park and multi-use trail in 1996. With the help of federal funding, the D.E.P. and crews from the towns of E. Hampton, Colchester, and Hebron began the process of clearing trees and debris, refurbishing the bridges, and resurfacing the rail bed with a 10-foot-wide surface of stone dust.

RULES OF THE TRAIL:

Bicyclists are requested to keep to the right side and pass on the left after audibly signaling. Give a friendly greeting before passing others from behind to avoid startling

153

them. When encountering horses, cyclists should stop at the side of the trail and wait for the horseback rider's instructions before proceeding.

Visitors should note that regulated hunting is permitted along much of the trail. Most hunting occurs between mid-October and late-December, with the exception of Sundays when it is prohibited by state law. Wear flourescent orange clothing if possible during this period.

Authorities remind all visitors not to block trailhead gates when parking since work crews and emergency vehicles always need access. Pets should be leashed, camping is prohibited, and the park is open from sunrise to sunset.

ORIENTATION:

This description covers the southern leg of the Airline State Park Trail from E. Hampton in the southwest to Hebron in the northeast. Undeveloped portions of the trail extend from both of these endpoints with rougher conditions. Other portions of the Airline State Park Trail are detailed in chapters 25 and 26.

Parking lots are provided at the E. Hampton end and at Rte. 2 (Exit 16). Smaller, roadside parking spots are present at most of the other road intersections. The trail's lowest elevation is near its midpoint at the crossing of the Salmon River and higher elevations exist at each endpoint. Since the area is relatively remote when compared to some of the state's other multi-use trails, cyclists are urged to be self-sufficient in their food, water, and bike tools.

TRAIL DESCRIPTION:

Starting at the E. Hampton trailhead on **Smith St.**, the Airline follows the shore of a small pond and then enters the shade of woods on a broad, righthand turn toward the southeast which passes the back yards of a few residences. It soon develops a faint downhill slope which lasts for most of the next 4.7 miles to the Salmon River, allowing an easy start for cyclists but requiring extra effort on the return ride.

The trail passes through a long cut in the bedrock of a hill and emerges at the start of the **Rapallo Viaduct** at the 1.3-mile mark. Named for a railroad director, the high, quarter-mile-long earthen causeway was originally a 60-foot-tall bridge built over **Flat Brook** in 1873 but was filled in 1913 in order to accommodate heavier trains. Steel portions of the original bridge protrude at points along the trail surface. The viaduct provides an excellent view over a wetland to the north but visitors are urged to use appropriate caution along its high, steep bankings.

The trail enters woods on the other side and soon passes the boundary for **Salmon River State Forest**, a 6,115-acre property which is popular for hunting and fishing. The state forest protects the next few miles of scenery, some of the trail's best.

Near the 2.3-mile mark the Airline Trail turns back to the east, crosses the Colchester town line, and approaches the **Lyman Viaduct** at the 2.6-mile mark. Named after the railroad's first president, this larger viaduct also originated as a bridge in 1873 and was filled in 1913 to accommodate heavier trains. Parts of the original steel structure remain visible above the fill as reminders of the huge structure now buried in gravel. The trail surface stands about 140 feet above **Dickinson Brook** at the bottom of the valley and allows unbroken views to the north and south.

The Airline reaches a small parking area at a sharp, hairpin corner on **Bull Hill Rd.** after 3.1 miles. It then turns in a northeasterly direction and continues with a gentle downslope through a hilly terrain of cuts and fills in the valley of the **Salmon River**. The rail bed is confined to a shelf along a slope in the narrow valley with walls of exposed bedrock and the evergreen foliage of mountain laurel lining the edges. **River Rd.**, barely visible through the forest, parallels at a lower elevation and passes through a stone arch bridge underneath the trail at the 4.7-mile mark.

A bridge carries the Airline Trail high over the Salmon River shortly beyond River Rd.'s stone arch bridge and the

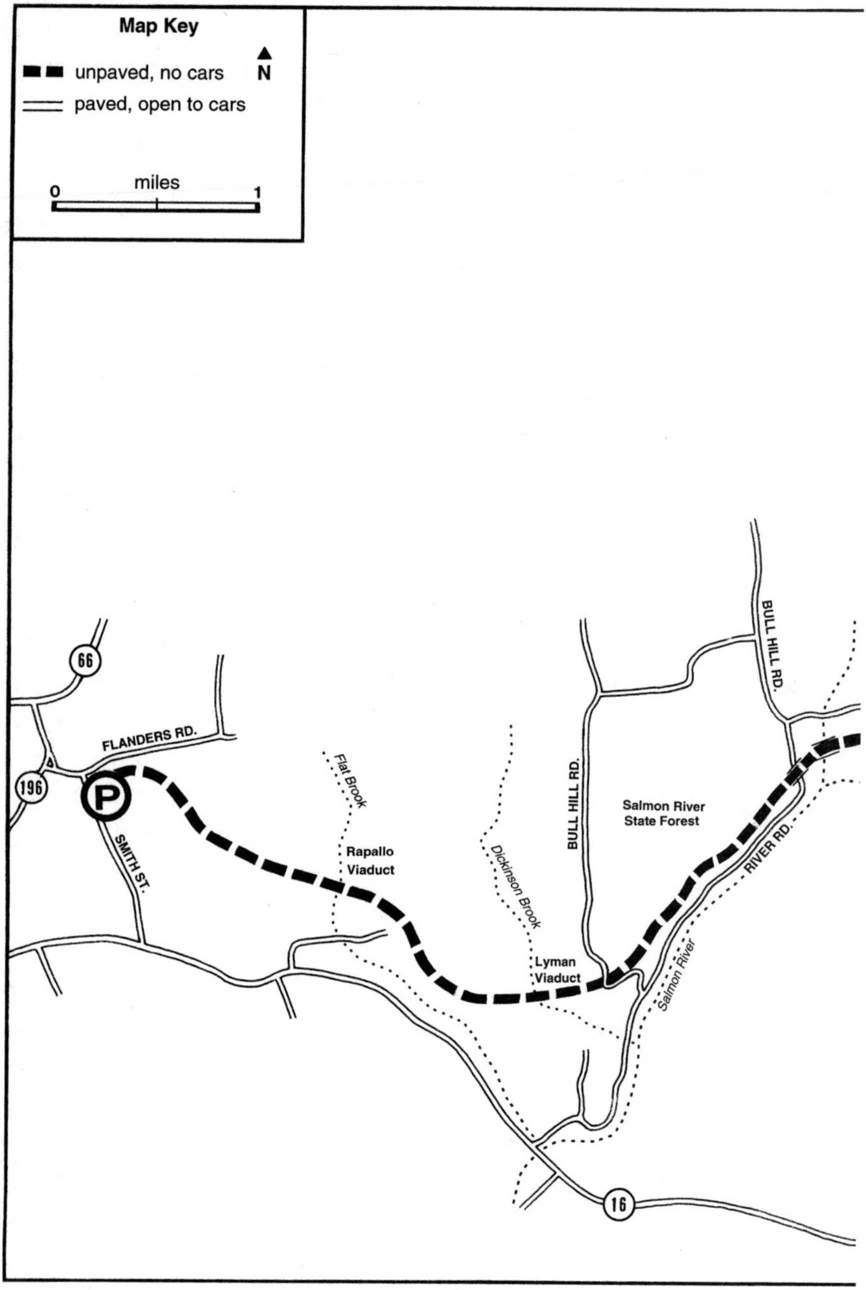

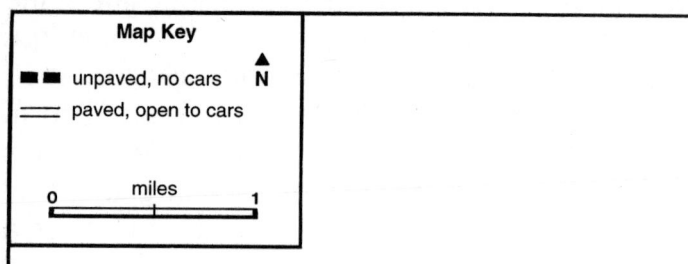

Map Key

▬ ▬ unpaved, no cars

═══ paved, open to cars

▲ N

0 ———— miles ———— 1

66

FLANDERS RD.

196

P

SMITH ST.

Flat Brook

Rapallo
Viaduct

Dickinson Brook

BULL HILL RD.

Salmon River
State Forest

BULL HILL RD.

RIVER RD.

Salmon River

Lyman
Viaduct

16

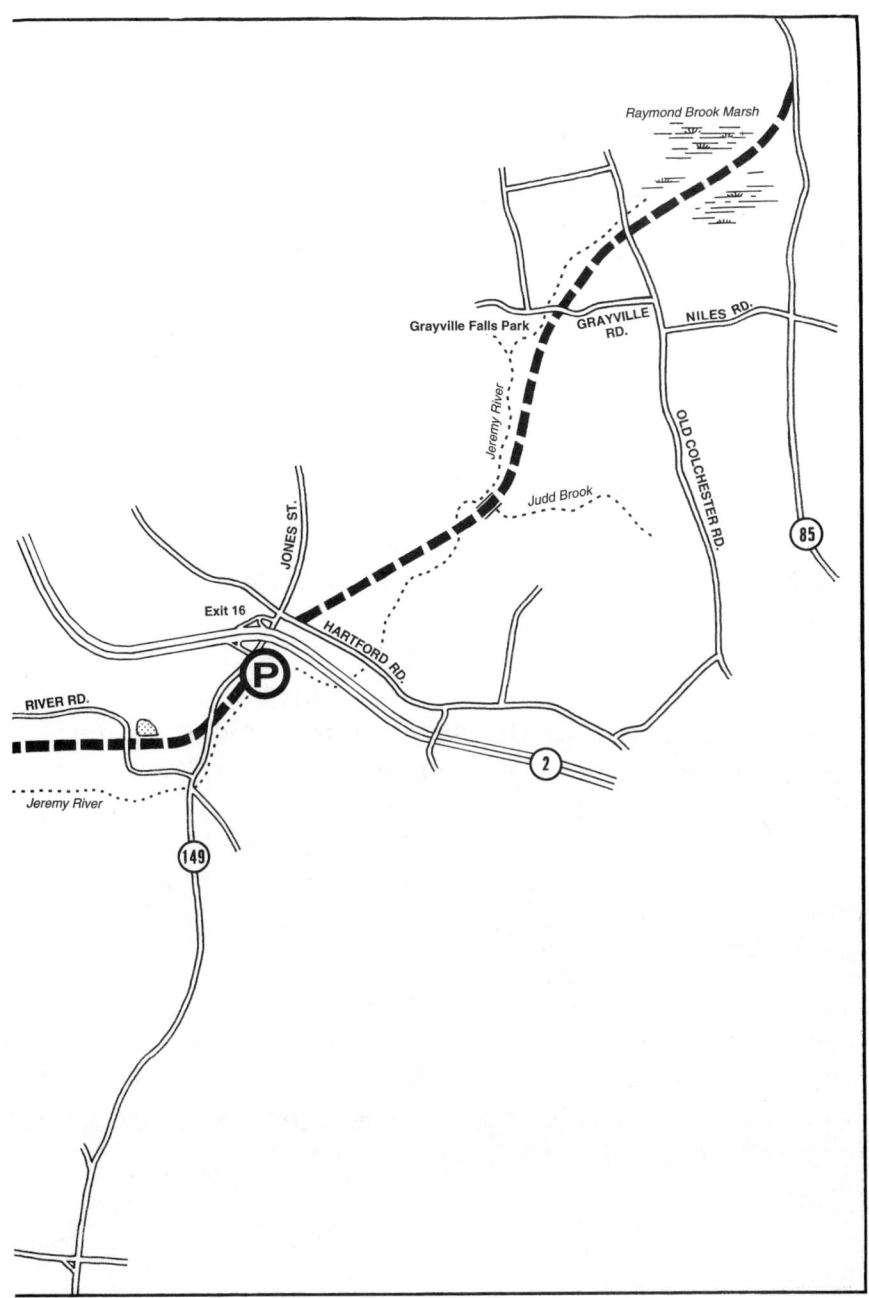

trail leaves the state forest heading east on a mile-long straightaway. A slight uphill grade develops at this point. The trail crosses River Rd. again at the 5.5-mile mark and turns back to the northeast at **Rte. 149** where it follows the valley of **Jeremy River** to the Park & Ride lot beside **Rte. 2** (Exit 16) at the 6.4-mile mark.

To continue, riders must detour for a third of a mile on roads because the rail line was obstructed by the creation of the highway. Follow Rte. 149 underneath Rte. 2, turn right on **Old Hartford Rd.**, then look for the trail at a yellow gate on the left.

The trail resumes with a mostly flat, straight course for the next 0.9 miles to a bridge over Jeremy River where it tilts upward on a slight slope. Turning to the north and crossing a bridge over **Judd Brook**, it enters the town of Hebron and straightens on a mile-long uphill grade beside **Grayville Falls Park**, a town-owned preserve with trails, a waterfall, and picnic areas.

Crossing **Grayville Rd.** at the 8.9-mile mark, the trail reaches flat ground and follows a corridor of trees for the next half-mile to **Old Colchester Rd.** Young hardwoods have encroached along the shoulders of the rail bed giving it a narrower feel along this stretch even though its smooth surface of stone dust remains about 10 feet wide.

The last 1.2 miles ranks among the Airline's most scenic. The trail emerges from the shade of trees in the open area of **Raymond Brook Marsh**, a large open wetland which allows a distant view and the possibility of seeing a variety of birdlife and wildlife. It traverses the marsh on a low, half-mile-long causeway and then returns to the woods for the last half-mile to **Rte. 85**, where the developed portion of the trail ends after 10.7 miles.

DRIVING DIRECTIONS:

To reach the E. Hampton trailhead from Rte. 2, take Exit 13 and follow Rte. 66 west for 4.2 miles. Turn left on Rte. 196 south and drive for 0.4 miles, then turn left on Flanders Rd. Continue for a quarter-mile, turn right on Smith St., then look for the parking lot on the left beside the pond.

TOILET FACILITIES:

None provided

BIKE SHOPS:

Cycle Escape, 50 Main St., Hebron, (860) 228-2453

Sunshine Cycle & Sport, 467 S. Main St., Colchester,
(860) 537-2788

ADDITIONAL INFORMATION:

Connecticut Dept. of Environmental Protection, 79 Elm St., Hartford, CT 06106-5127, Tel. (860) 424-3200

web: http://dep.state.ct.us

25
Airline State Park Trail
Windham - Pomfret

length: 19.6 miles
surface: mostly hard-packed gravel
terrain: gentle slopes

This section of the Airline rail-trail ventures into rural scenery of farmland and forests. Given the trail's rough surfaces in places, riders should use mountain bikes or wide-tired hybrids.

BACKGROUND:

The trail follows the route of the Air Line Railroad, built in 1873 on an "air-line" between New York and Boston. Since it bypassed Connecticut's capitol, construction of a direct route between the two cities faced political controversy as well as natural obstacles including a crossing of the Connecticut River and a rough topography. The Air Line's relatively hilly, curvey profile eventually restricted its success as trains began to carry heavier loads and opted for flatter routes. A flood in 1955 destroyed the railroad's bridge over the Quinebaug River and it was never rebuilt.

Following the line's abandonment, the Connecticut Dept. of Transportation acquired much of the route and transferred management of the property to the Dept. of Environmental Protection.

RULES OF THE TRAIL:

Bicyclists are asked to ride at a safe speed and give a friendly greeting before passing others from behind to avoid startling them. When encountering horses, stop at the side of the trail and wait for the horseback rider's instructions before proceeding.

Visitors should note that regulated hunting is permitted along much of the trail. Most hunting occurs between mid-October and late December with the exception of Sundays, when it is prohibited by state law. Wear flourescent orange clothing if possible during this period.

Authorities remind trail users not to block trailhead gates when parking since work crews and emergency vehicles always need access. Motorized vehicles are prohibited. The park is open from sunrise to sunset.

ORIENTATION:

The trail extends in a northeast direction from Rte. 66 near Willimantic to Wrights Crossing Rd. in Pomfret. Parking is available at a gravel turnout beside the intersection of Lynch and Chewink roads in Chaplin, or at Goodwin State Forest in Hampton where there are also toilets. Limited space for roadside parking exists at other trail/road intersections. The highest elevation on this section of the trail is near its midpoint at Station Rd. in Hampton and the lowest points are near the trail's endpoints.

This section of the Airline State Park Trail has not been formally developed but its condition is adequate for riding a mountain or hybrid bicycle. Crushed stone smoothens a few sections but most of the surface consists of hard-packed gravel which is bumpy in places. Gates block vehicles from entering at road intersections but no crosswalks or other safety features exist. Since the trail reaches remote areas, be sure that your bike is in good repair and bring adequate amounts of water and food when planning a long ride.

TRAIL DESCRIPTION:

Goodwin State Forest in Hampton makes one of the best starting points for a ride on the Airline Tr. A parking lot, toilets, nature center, picnic area, and view over **Pine Acres Lake** lend a peaceful atmosphere to the surroundings. To reach the trail from the parking lot, turn right on **Potter Rd.** and continue for a quarter-mile.

Turn left on the Airline State Park Tr. to reach the southwest endpoint near Willimantic, 7.1 miles away. A slight downhill pitch is present for most of this distance. The ride begins with a half-mile straightaway to a bridge where the trail and a small brook pass underneath **Rte. 6**, then turns through a cut in a hillside. Crushed stone forms a smooth surface for this first section. The trail reaches the intersection of **S. Brook Rd.** and **Parker Rd.** at about the 1-mile mark and continues downhill with a slightly bumpier surface through forest scenery for the next 1.9 miles.

It descends a short slope to cross **Chewink Rd.** in Chaplin at the site of a missing bridge at the 2.9-mile mark. A gravel turnout at this point provides additional trailhead parking. It continues west for the next mile in an area of stone walls beside **Lynch Rd.** at the foot of **Beaver Hill**, then rounds a corner heading southwest into Windham.

The trail crosses a wooden bridge over **Boulevard Rd.** and descends another banking at a missing bridge over **Rte. 203** at the 5.1-mile mark. Here a sign marks the **Windham Atlantic White Cedar Bog** which is owned by Joshua's Trust, a private land conservation organization. The bog is visible ahead on the right side of the trail.

The remaining 2 miles have a variety of conditions. The gentle downslope flattens at the bog and reverses to a gradual incline upon reaching the other side. A quarter-mile after passing the end of **Crystal Rd.**, the trail's gravel surface changes to pavement and it turns left where the on- and off-ramps for a Rte. 6 interchange block the straight course of the original rail line. The paved trail climbs a steeper slope alongside the highway ramps and then descends beside **Tuckie Rd.** to **Rte. 66**.

Riding from Potter Rd. at Goodwin State Forest to the Airline's northeast endpoint at Wrights Crossing Rd. is a 12.5-mile adventure (one-way). The first couple of miles are uphill and the remaining ten are either flat or gentle downhill.

Heading north from Potter Rd. in Hampton, the trail rises on a mile-long straightaway above Pine Acres Lake which is visible through the trees once the leaves have fallen. Brush has been cleared from the sides of the rail bed along this section giving it a wide look. The trail makes a brief descent to the crossing of **Estabrook Rd.**, climbs back

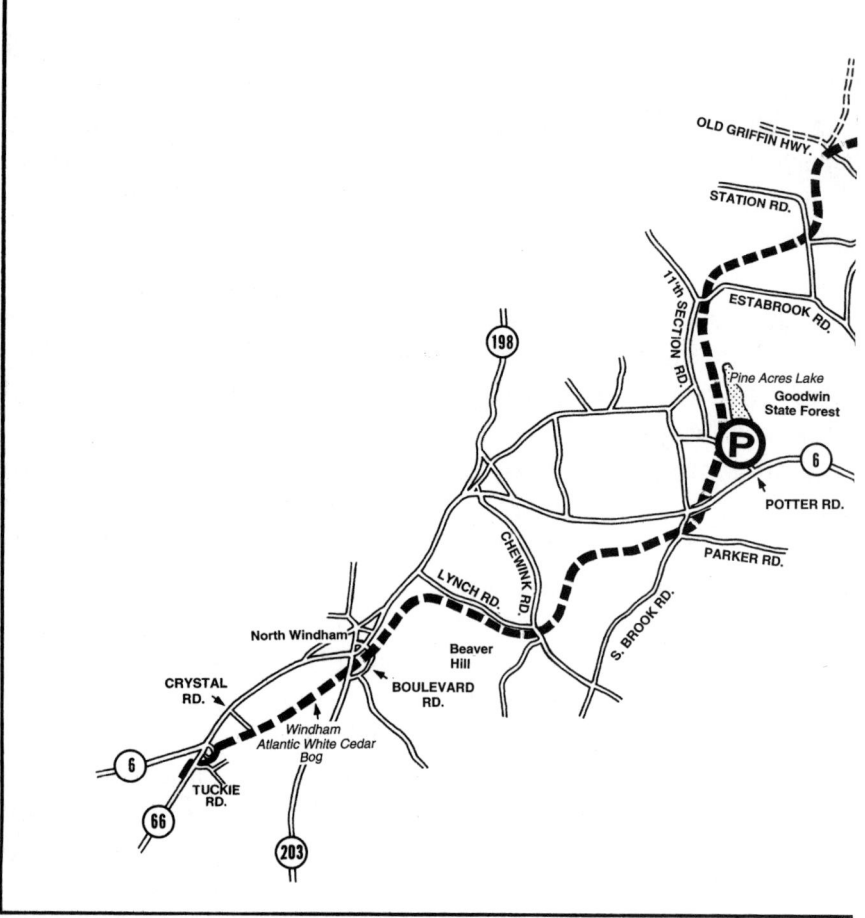

OLD GRIFFIN HWY.

STATION RD.

11th SECTION RD.

ESTABROOK RD.

198

Pine Acres Lake
Goodwin
State Forest

P

6

POTTER RD.

CHEWINK RD.

LYNCH RD.

PARKER RD.

S. BROOK RD.

North Windham

Beaver
Hill

CRYSTAL
RD.

BOULEVARD
RD.

*Windham
Atlantic White Cedar
Bog*

6

TUCKIE
RD.

66

203

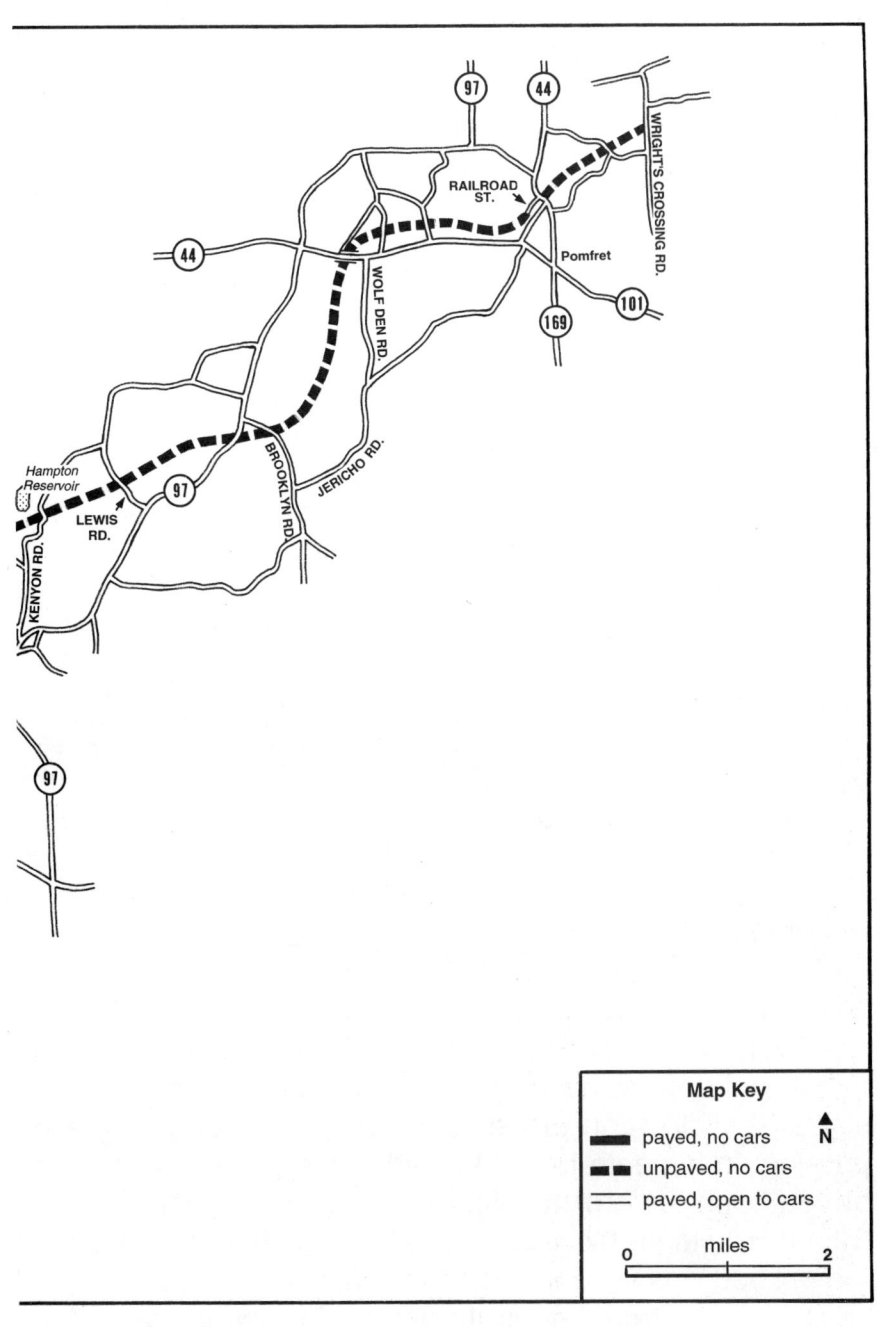

to the railroad grade, and turns eastward on a high earthen causeway built over a low-lying area. An even surface of crushed stone and gravel provides smooth rolling here.

The uphill pitch flattens somewhat as the trail enters an area of marshland 2.3-miles from Potter Rd. It reaches its highest elevation at **Station Rd.** after 2.8 miles where a clearing and cluster of houses marks one of the former railroad's many stopping points. Turning northward again, the trail returns to woods with a slight downslope that lasts for most of the remaining distance. After passing a nature sanctuary of the Connecticut Audubon Society on the right, the trail follows a causeway over Hampton Brook and turns back to the northeast before crossing **Old Griffin Hwy.** at the 3.8-mile mark.

The trail straightens as it passes south of **Hampton Reservoir** and crosses **Kenyon Rd.** after a half-mile. Several farm fields open the scenery along the next 0.9 miles to **Lewis Rd.** where the rail bed has been filled and trail users must scramble up a banking to cross the street.

Encroaching tree branches and a grassy surface in places give the trail's remaining distance a less-used appearance. A few wet spots slow the pedaling along the next 1.3 miles to **Rte. 97** where the trail enters Pomfret, and the surface is flat and grassy for the next third of a mile to another cluster of houses at **Brooklyn Rd.**, 6.8 miles from Potter Rd. Here a rock sits beside the trail and is inscribed, Elliott Station, marking another former train stop.

The trail rounds Easter Hill after this point and heads northward alongside its rocky slope on a 2-mile leg through forest and marshland to the first crossing of **Rte. 44.** Few signs of civilization are evident along this stretch. After passing underneath Rte. 44 beside Abington Brook, the trail bends back toward the east and meets Osgood Rd. and Babbit Hill Rd. in the next mile, climbing short slopes where the rail bed was filled at each road crossing.

The trail continues its gentle downward run for the next 1.2 miles and then passes a trailhead gate at the 11.1-

mile mark, joins a gravel driveway, and veers left off the rail bed to reach **Railroad St.** Follow Railroad St. downhill to Rte. 44, turn right, and look for the trail to resume on the left at a gravel turnout. A former bridge once carried the railroad over the street at this location.

Lack of use has narrowed the treadway to a footpath along the last 1.2 miles to Wrights Crossing Rd. but the surface is mostly smooth. It begins on another high causeway built across a wetland, cuts through a hillside, and then drops abruptly to cross Needles Eye Rd. The final half mile to **Wright's Crossing Rd.** passes the Bafflin Sanctuary, another property of the Connecticut Audubon Society.

Here the beaten path ends, 12.5 miles from Potter Rd. at Goodwin State Forest. The rail bed continues to the northeast but is obstructed by forest debris and suffers from drainage problems.

DRIVING DIRECTIONS:

To reach Goodwin State Forest from I-395, take Exit 91W and follow Rte. 6 west for 12.3 miles. Turn right on Potter Rd. and look for the parking lot on the right. Follow Potter Rd. for another quarter-mile to reach the trail.

To reach the Lynch Rd./Chewink Rd. parking lot, continue on Rte. 6 west for another 4 miles. Turn left at a traffic signal on Lynch Rd. and drive 1.4 miles to the end, then look for the gravel turnout on the right.

Heading east on Rte. 6, find Lynch Rd. on the right 1.1 miles past the intersection of Rte. 203, or continue for another 4 miles to Potter Rd. on the left.

TOILET FACILITIES:

Toilets are available at Goodwin State Forest.

BIKE SHOPS:

Alternative Spoke,15 Phelps Way, Willington, (860) 487-6100
Al's Ordinary Bike Shop, 21 Furnace St., Danielson, (860) 774-1660
Rainbow Cycle, 385 Valley St., Willimantic, (860) 423-7182
Scott's Cyclery, 1171 Main St., Willimantic, (860) 423-8889
Silver Bicycle, 6 Livery St., Putnam, (860) 928-7370

ADDITIONAL INFORMATION:

Connecticut Dept. of Environmental Protection, 79 Elm St., Hartford, CT 06106-5127, Tel. (860) 424-3200
web: http://dep.state.ct.us

26
Airline State Park Trail
Thompson - Douglas, MA

length: 7.7 miles to Douglas State Forest
surface: gravel, either rough or soft in places
terrain: gentle slopes

The Airline's northernmost leg has some of its most difficult conditions so cyclists should be prepared with either a mountain bike or wide-tired hybrid. The trail crosses the Massachusetts border and continues as the Southern New England Trunk Line Trail reaching Douglas State Forest and other points east.

BACKGROUND:

The Airline State Park Trail follows the path of the former Air Line Railroad, named for the fact that it was laid on a direct line between Boston and New York. Bypassing Hartford, the route was famous for its fast passenger trains but its relatively hilly, curvey profile eventually restricted its success as trains began to carry heavier loads and opted for flatter routes. A flood in 1955 destroyed the railroad's bridge over the Quinebaug River in Putnam and it was never rebuilt.

Following the line's abandonment, the Connecticut Dept. of Transportation acquired much of the route and transferred management of the property to the Dept. of Environmental Protection.

This chapter describes the Airline State Park Trail from Thompson to the Massachusetts state line, and the Southern New England Trunk Line Trail from the state line to Douglas State Forest. The Southern New England Trunk Line Trail continues to Franklin, MA but missing or decrepit bridges cause disruptions at several points east of Uxbridge. Both the Connecticut and Massachusetts portions of the trail have not been developed with an improved surface or official trailhead parking lots.

RULES OF THE TRAIL:

Bicyclists should keep to the right, pass on the left, and give a friendly greeting to others when approaching from behind to avoid startling them. Use extra caution when encountering horses by stopping at the side of the trail and waiting for the instructions of the horseback rider before proceeding.

Hunting is popular in this area from mid-October to late December when deer season is underway. During this period, visitors are advised to wear blaze orange clothing if possible or to ride on Sundays, when hunting is prohibited by state law in both Connecticut and Massachusetts.

ORIENTATION:

The Airline State Park Trail is aligned in the southwest-to-northeast direction. Although numerous road crossings exist, many do not allow easy access to the trail and few have space for parking. The best starting point for the Connecticut portion of the trail is a turnout on East Thompson Rd. in Thompson and the best starting point for the Massachusetts portion is Douglas State Forest in Douglas.

The trail is completely undeveloped so signs, crosswalks, and other safety features do not exist. Gates are in place to prevent motor vehicle entry but off-road motorcycle usage has worn the trail surface in places and created the "wash board" effect of up-and-down berms. In general, the roughest conditions are found intermittently along the Connecticut portion while the Massachusetts section has a smoother surface.

TRAIL DESCRIPTION:

Starting at **East Thompson Rd.** and heading southwest, cyclists can ride for about 5 miles to Rte. 200. The trip starts with a short climb up a scrabbly slope at the site of a former bridge which carried trains above the road. Here the trail continues across a wide, gravelly area which is rippled with a wave-like pattern of motorcycle berms, then

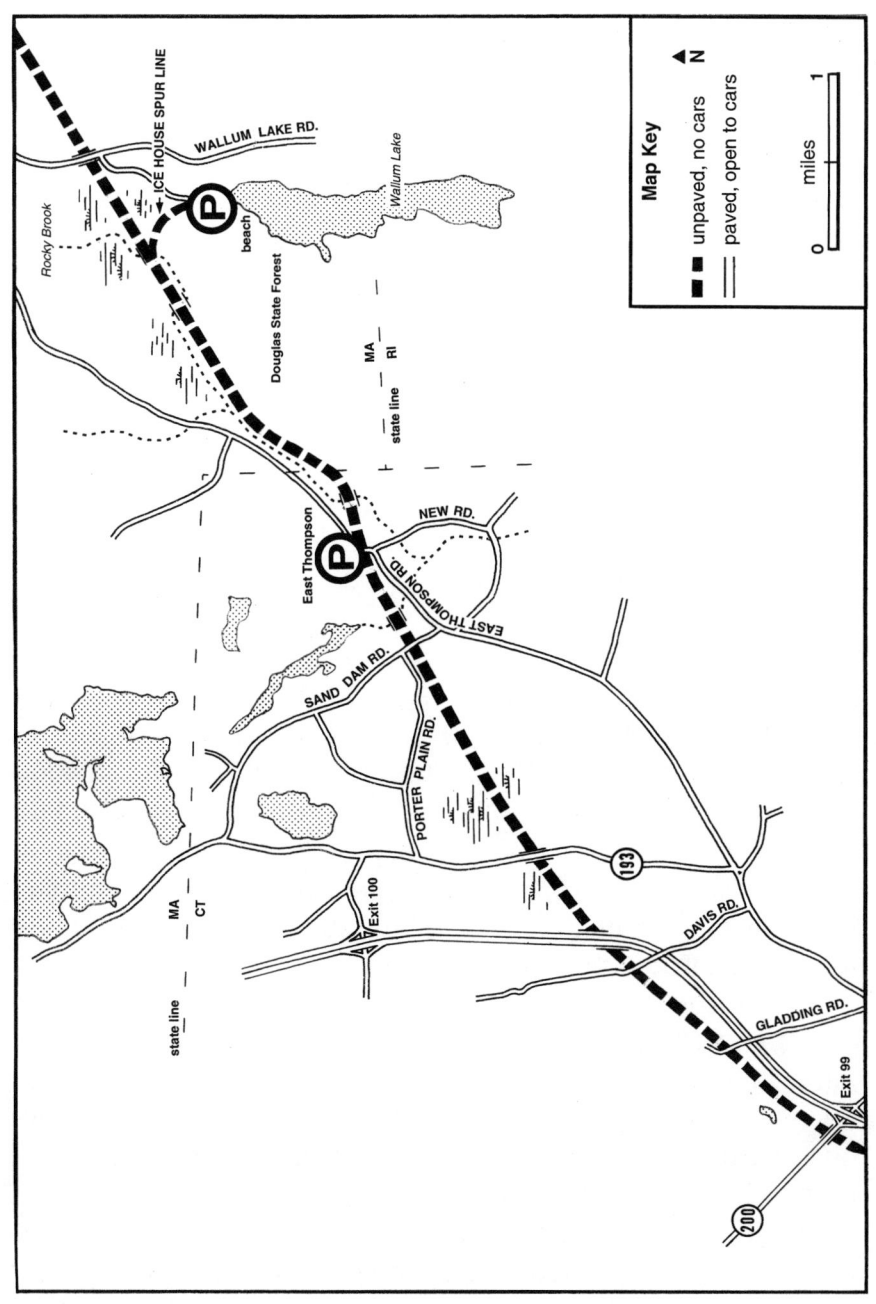

enters nearby woods with a smoother surface and narrower space. After a half-mile it passes between two ponds and narrows from encroaching tree branches before scrambling up a banking at the crossing of **Sand Dam Rd.**

The next mile and a half are straight and flat but berms slow some portions of the trail with a rollercoaster of tiny ups and downs. Part of this distance follows an earthen causeway through a large wetland. On the other side, a short detour loops around a rotting bridge over a former cattle crossing. Carefully crafted stone walls appear along both sides of the rail bed for the next several miles as reminders of the past when the surrounding acreage was active farmland.

The trail continues underneath a bridge for **Rte. 193** at the 2.1-mile mark and then under two bridges carrying **I-395** at the 2.7-mile mark. Noise from the highway remains noticeable from the trail as it parallels the interstate for the remaining distance to Rte. 200.

Most of the next mile has a slight uphill grade. The trail climbs a banking on another short detour where fill used for **Gladding Rd.** blocks the rail bed and, a half-mile beyond, a final detour loops past another decrepit bridge over a cattle crossing. The trail passes underneath **Rte. 200** at the 4.6-mile mark and descends toward the Quinebaug River but conditions for biking degrade. Within a half-mile, drainage problems plague the trail surface and it becomes an eroded stream bed of rocks, mud, and water.

Heading in the northeast direction from East Thompson Rd., the trail extends into Massachusetts. The first quarter-mile follows a straight, narrow corridor through the woods. After passing underneath an old wooden bridge, the trail surface degrades with loose sand and a series of berms which slow the pedaling for the next 0.4 miles to the Massachusetts state line, where a metal gate marks the border and a sign reads, "No motorized vehicles."

Here it is known as the **Southern New England Trunk Line Trail** and conditions get smoother. A hard-packed finish of crushed stone and gravel eases the rolling as the trail rises on a gradual, half-mile slope beside **Rocky Brook** and enters 5,000-acre **Douglas State Forest**. It then crosses a wooden bridge over a tributary stream and straightens on a 2-mile line through a string of open wetlands with interesting scenery on both sides.

After 2.3 miles from E. Thompson Rd., look for a spur trail branching on the right (southeast) side. Known as the **Ice House Spur Line**, this rail-trail connects the Douglas State Forest access road near the swimming beach at **Wallum Lake**.

DRIVING DIRECTIONS:
To reach the East Thompson Rd. trailhead from I-395, take Exit 99 and follow Rte. 200 east to Thompson center. Turn left on Rte. 193 north and drive for 1.5 miles, then fork right on East Thompson Rd. After 2.5 miles, fork right at Sand Dam Rd. and continue on East Thompson Rd. for another 0.6 miles, then look for the gravel turnout at an S-turn. Park well off the road, being careful not to block access to the gate.

To reach Douglas State Forest in Douglas, MA, follow I-395 north into Massachusetts and take Exit 2. Follow Rte. 16 east for 5.3 miles, turn right on Cedar St. and drive for 0.8 miles to the end, then continue straight on Wallum Lake Rd. Look for the park entrance on the right after 0.9 miles.

TOILET FACILITIES:
Available (in season) at Douglas State Forest.

BIKE SHOPS:
Blackstone Canal Bicycles, 2 S. Main St., Uxbridge, MA,
(508) 278-3080
Mottola Bicycle, 24 Sayles Ave., Burrilleville, RI, (401) 568-2228
Silver Bicycle, 6 Livery St., Putnam, (860) 928-7370

ADDITIONAL INFORMATION:
Connecticut Dept. of Environmental Protection, 79 Elm St., Hartford, CT 06106-5126, Tel. (860) 424-3200,
web: http://dep.state.ct.us

Douglas State Forest, 108 Wallum Lake Rd., Douglas, MA 01516, Tel. (508) 476-7872

27
Putnam River Trail
Putnam

length: 1 mile
surface: paved
terrain: small slopes

Located in the center of town, the Putnam River Trail is a safe haven for local walkers, in-line skaters, kids on bikes, and others looking for smooth, car-free pavement. Excellent views of the Quinebaug River await at points along the way.

BACKGROUND:

The origin of the Putnam River Trail lies in a natural disaster. Following a severe hurricane in August, 1955, the Quinebaug River overflowed its banks and caused extensive damage to many of downtown Putnam's factories and businesses. In the years that followed, a redevelopment effort included construction of new roads, housing, and a shopping center, as well as the creation of Rotary Park where the trail is now located.

Today the park and its new trail are a proud centerpiece for the town. Adorned with lawns, plantings, lamp poles, and interpretive historical signs, the trail draws townspeople outside to enjoy the Quinebaug and its scenic riverbank. It was dedicated in 1998 to the citizens of Putnam who have worked to improve the community.

RULES OF THE TRAIL:

Bicyclists are asked to share the trail with others. Yield to pedestrians, ride at a safe speed, keep to the right side, and pass on the left. Alert others before passing from behind to avoid startling them. The trail's downtown location creates mostly pedestrian use so cyclists are urged to be cautious and courteous. The trail is open from dawn to dusk.

The Putnam River Trail follows a strip of greenspace between the Quinebaug River and Kennedy Dr. It extends for a mile between the Arch St. Bridge in the south and Bridge St. in the north, then continues as a bike lane on Kennedy Dr. for another third of a mile to Miller Park. At three points the trail briefly joins the edge of Kennedy Dr. as a sidewalk but the remaining portion of the trail is completely separated from the road. It crosses two streets in the downtown area and each has a crosswalk with a traffic signal control.

Four public parking lots are located beside the trail with the largest being located near the Arch St. Bridge at the southern end. This parking lot is shown on the trail map and is the recommended starting point for cyclists. Visitors will find picnic tables, benches, and trash cans at various points along the trail.

TRAIL DESCRIPTION:

Starting at the southernmost parking lot, the trail heads southward for only a short distance, first on a sidewalk beside **Kennedy Dr.** and then on a newly built pedestrian/bicycle bridge over the **Quinebaug River**. Allowing a good view over the water, this bridge occupies the site of the former **Arch St. Bridge**, a high railroad span which was destroyed in the 1955 flood and caused the closing of the Airline Railroad between New York and Boston.

Heading north from the parking lot, the trail meanders through an area where picnic tables, shade trees, and a good view of the river invite people to stop and sit. It follows the road at a distance as it curves with a bend in the river, then merges beside a guardrail as the park squeezes through a tight area between the roadway and the water. After separating at a second parking lot, the trail follows a short section of sidewalk beside the road where a wooden fence protects a steep banking above the river. It passes a third parking area and then rises on a short slope to the

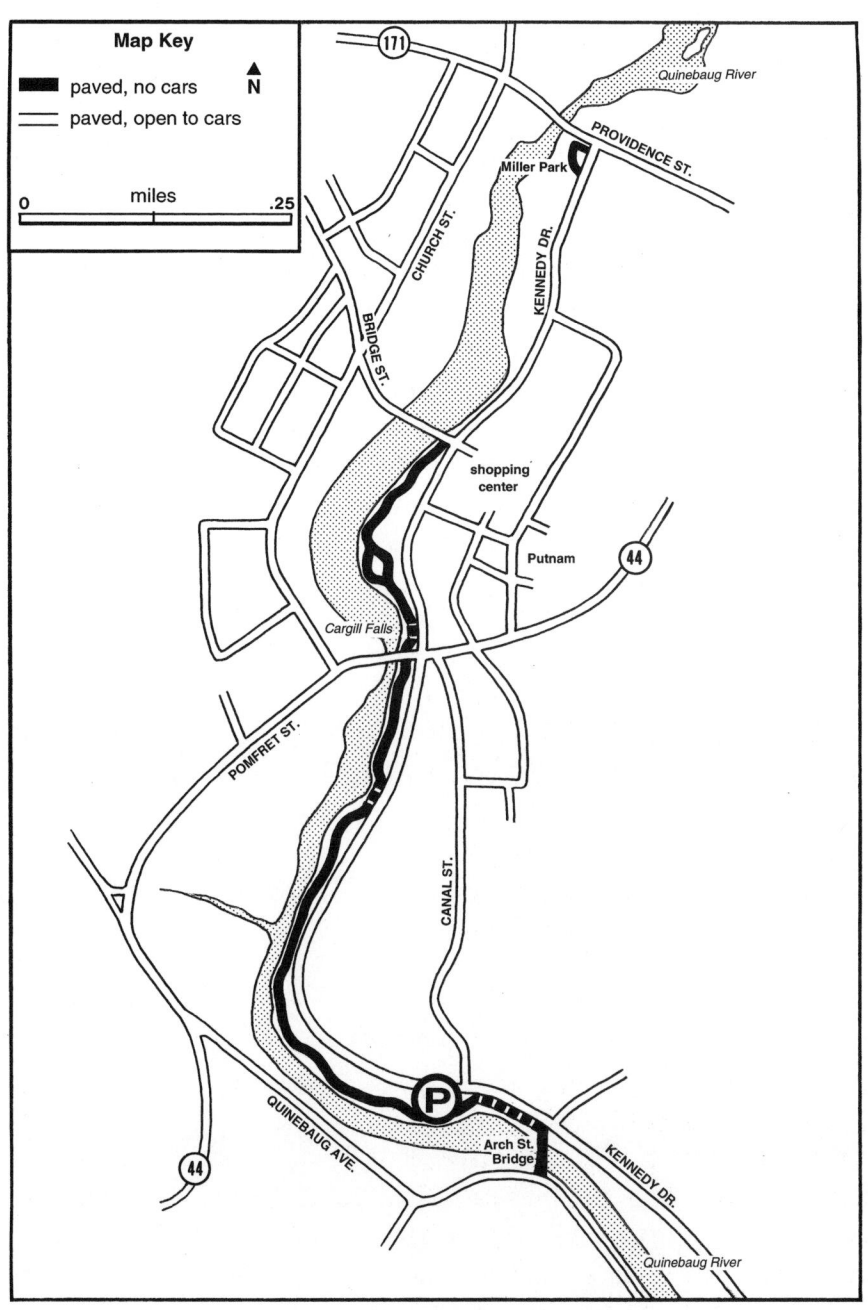

Map Key

■■■ paved, no cars

— paved, open to cars

N

0 ____ miles ____ .25

171

Quinebaug River

PROVIDENCE ST.

Miller Park

CHURCH ST.

KENNEDY DR.

BRIDGE ST.

shopping center

Putnam

44

Cargill Falls

POMFRET ST.

CANAL ST.

P

QUINEBAUG AVE.

Arch St. Bridge

KENNEDY DR.

44

Quinebaug River

intersection of **Pomfret St. (Rte. 44)**.

Crossing to the north side of the street, the trail offers a good view of **Cargill Falls** where the Quinebaug tumbles off a ledgy drop. It follows a third stretch of sidewalk beside Kennedy Dr. and then turns away from the road and rises on a slight slope to a rock outcropping where several memorials are located, including one recognizing Rotary International for its assistance after the 1955 flood. The trail continues over flat ground along a line of lamp poles at the edge of the river to **Bridge St.**, where it ends.

A bike lane painted on both sides of Kennedy Dr. extends the riding northward for another third of a mile to **Miller Park**, where a small greenspace and an information kiosk are located at the corner of **Providence St. (Rte. 171)**.

DRIVING DIRECTIONS:

From I-395 take Exit 95 and follow Kennedy Dr. north toward Putnam for about three quarters of a mile. Look for the parking lot on the left beside the river, just after a high, stone bridge abuttment on the right.

TOILET FACILITIES:

None provided on the trail.

BIKE SHOPS:

Silver Bicycle, 6 Livery St., Putnam, (860) 928-7370

28
Quinebaug River Trail
Killingly

length: 1 mile
surface: paved
terrain: gentle slopes

This short ribbon of asphalt connects the cramped streets of Danielson with peaceful scenery along the Quinebaug River. Proposed extensions will hopefully make it a much longer route.

BACKGROUND:

The Quinebaug River Trail's origins lie with a state highway reconstruction project in Danielson. When the rotary intersection of Rte. 6 and Rte. 12 was reconfigured with a traffic signal in 1991, extra space along the Quinebaug River was utilized for a park and pathway. The path doubled in length in 1995 when it was extended southward through town-owned lands with the help of federal funding. Local planners hope to continue the trail's progress southward along an old trolley line toward the neighboring town of Plainfield.

RULES OF THE TRAIL:

Bicyclists are requested to yield to pedestrians and should give a warning before passing them to avoid any surprises. Help keep the area litter-free by carrying out at least as much as you carry in. The trail is open only during daylight hours.

ORIENTATION:

The 10-foot-wide paved trail runs in the north-to-south direction. A trailhead parking lot is located across Rte. 6/Rte. 12 from the northern end, with crosswalks and signal controls providing safe passage across the roadway. Additional parking is available near the south end of the trail at the ball field complex off Rte. 12.

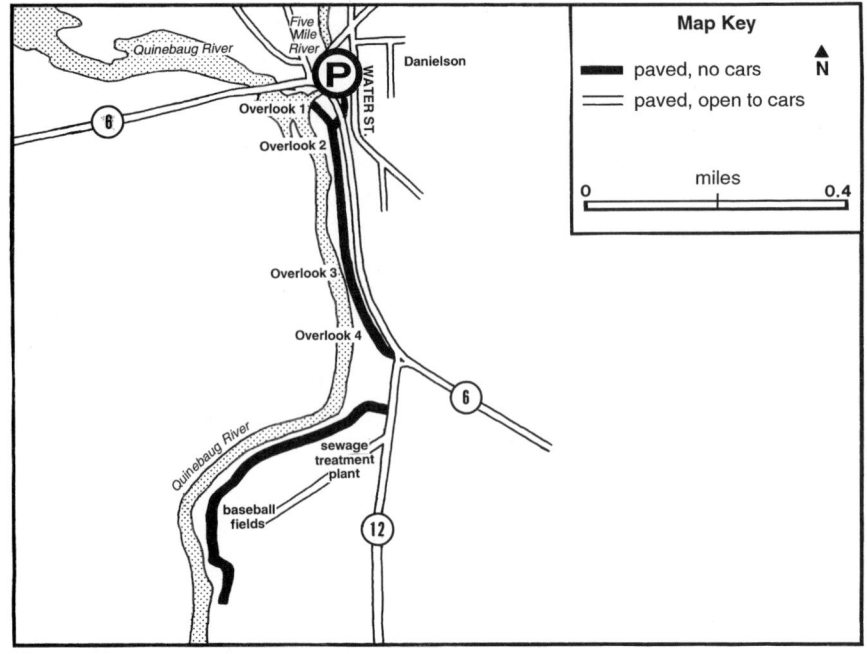

The first section of trail parallels the roadway at a safe distance, then a short midsection utilizes a sidewalk beside Rte. 12, and the last section ventures away from any roads.

TRAIL DESCRIPTION:

From the parking lot off **Water St.**, follow the crosswalk across **Rte. 6/Rte. 12** to reach the trail at **Overlook 2**. Turning to the right, the Quinebaug River Tr. runs for only a short distance to **Overlook 1**, built above the confluence of the **Quinebaug River** and the **Five Mile River**. This overlook allows an excellent view over the water as well as a dam and canal which power a small hydroelectric station.

Heading south, the trail passes Overlook 2 in a strip of parkland between the river and the road. A decorative metal railing lines the trail along the edge of a steep slope above the river while plantings of trees and shrubs buffer the space between the road. A collection of benches and tables allows people to stop and rest. After passing **Overlook 3**, the trail's separation from the road narrows to a strip of grass and, after **Overlook 4**, it meets the roadway.

Turn right at this point and follow a sidewalk along Rte. 12 heading south. After a short distance, look for the trail to resume on the right, just before the town's **sewage treatment plant**. A sign marks the trail.

The trail runs west from this point, passing through a barricade which blocks vehicles from entering and then descending a slight slope behind the treatment plant. A wooden fence protects the trail where it approaches a banking above the river.

The trail soon emerges at a complex of **baseball fields** and circles the perimeter at the edge of the river before entering nearby woods where it turns through the trees for the remaining distance. It comes to a dead end at a secluded spot beside the water after almost a mile from the start.

DRIVING DIRECTIONS:
From I-395 take Exit 91W and follow Rte. 6 west to its junction with Rte. 12. Continue on Rte. 6 west/Rte. 12 north for a short distance to the next intersection, where the two split. Turn right on Rte. 12 north, then take the first right on Water St. Look for the "River Trail Parking" sign ahead on the right.
TOILET FACILITIES:
None are provided.
BIKE SHOPS:
Al's Ordinary Bike Shop, 21 Furnace St., Danielson, (860) 774-1660
ADDITIONAL INFORMATION:
Planning & Development, Town of Killingly, P.O. Box 6000, Killingly, CT 06239-6000, Tel. (860) 779-5311

Welcome to
MOOSUP VALLEY TRAIL
STATE PARK

This trail was once the right of
way for the New York New Haven
and Hartford Railroad Company
and is now part of the Rails To
Trails Program.

Please follow these simple rules:

Area closed at sunset.
Motorized vehicles and
rock collecting are prohibited.
Please keep this area clean.

29
Moosup Valley State Park Trail
Plainfield - Coventry, RI

length: 8.2 miles to the village of Greene, RI
surface: gravel that is loose or rough in places
terrain: flat

Crossing the state line and continuing as Rhode Island's Trestle Trail, this "undeveloped" rail-trail requires mountain or hybrid bikes. Its trailhead gateway is smooth with pavement but the remainder of the route has rough areas caused by off-road motorcycle usage.

BACKGROUND:

The Moosup Valley State Park Trail follows the bed of the former Hartford, Providence, and Fishkill Railroad which was organized in 1849 and completed in 1854. The line made a direct connection between the capitols of Connecticut and Rhode Island and provided prosperity for many small towns in between, including the mill village of Moosup.

Shortly after the tracks fell into disuse in the 1960's, the rails and ties were removed and the Connecticut Dept. of Transportation acquired the rail bed. Management of the route was transferred to the Dept. of Environmental Protection in 1987 and work began on clearing debris and constructing bridges for recreational use. Although more work remains to be done, the Moosup Valley State Park Trail links Rhode Island's Trestle Trail as part of the East Coast Greenway, a network of bike paths stretching from Maine to Florida.

RULES OF THE TRAIL:

Bicyclists are requested to yield to pedestrians and alert others before passing them. The trail is open from sunrise to sunset and is meant only for passive recreation, although motorbikes unfortunately make occasional use of it. All visitors are asked to help keep the area clean by carrying out what they carry in. Dogs must be leashed at all times.

Hunting is a popular activity in this area in the fall and early winter. Along the Connecticut portion of the trail cyclists are encouraged to wear blaze orange clothing (except on Sundays, when hunting is prohibited by state law). In Rhode Island, the Trestle Trail enters a wildlife management area where all visitors must wear at least 200 square inches of day-glo flourescent orange material as a hat or vest from the second Saturday in October to the last day of February.

ORIENTATION:

The Moosup Valley State Park Trail runs for 5.8 miles from the village of Moosup eastward to the Rhode Island state line where it becomes the Trestle Trail and continues eastward through Coventry. Although the starting point in Moosup has a paved surface and a trailhead sign, it is the only developed part of the trail and the remainder gets minimal maintenance. The Rhode Island portion is also undeveloped.

The trail's simple condition gives it the appearance of a gravel road but its flat course and long, even curves make it easy to recognize as a former rail line. Road crossings occur at regular intervals and help visitors plot their progress but few signs or other markings exist. The trail is relatively remote so do not expect to see many other trail users and be sure that your bike is in good working order.

TRAIL DESCRIPTION:

Starting beside mill buildings in the village of **Moosup**, the trail crosses the **Moosup River** on a railroad trestle bridge which has been retrofitted with wooden decking and protective fencing. The paved surface degrades to gravel on the other side and the trail follows a line of telephone poles paralleling **Whitney Hill Rd.** Exposed rocks and a few wet spots are among the avoidable obstacles for bicyclists along this stretch.

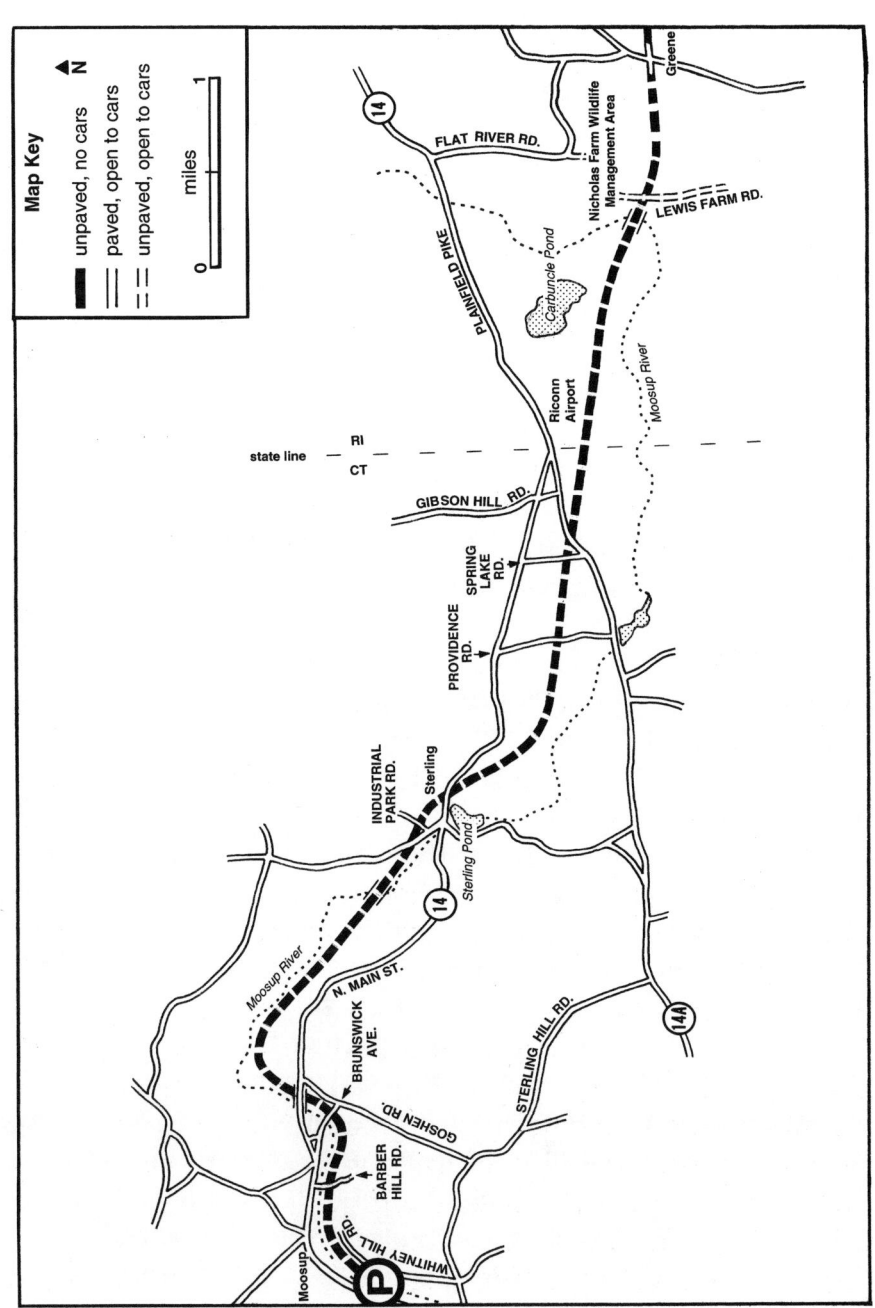

Map Key

■ unpaved, no cars
═ paved, open to cars
= = unpaved, open to cars

miles
0   1

N

FLAT RIVER RD.

PLANFIELD PIKE

Carbuncle Pond

Nicholas Farm Wildlife
Management Area

Greene

LEWIS FARM RD.

Riconn
Airport

Moosup River

state line — RI
          CT

GIBSON HILL RD.

SPRING
LAKE
RD.

PROVIDENCE
RD.

INDUSTRIAL
PARK RD.

Sterling

Sterling Pond

Moosup River

N. MAIN ST.

BRUNSWICK
AVE.

GOSHEN RD.

STERLING HILL RD.

BARBER
HILL RD.

WHITNEY HILL RD.

Moosup

14

14

14A

P

Conditions get smoother after the crossing of **Barber Hill Rd.** as the trail slips into forest shade and follows the river upstream. Look for Glen Falls at the 1.1-mile mark where the trail crosses **Brunswick Ave.** at another millsite.

It continues northward under a high bridge carrying **Rte. 14**, then makes a half-mile-long turn back to the southeast and straightens for over a mile through more woods to Sterling. The trail offers several pretty views of the Moosup River along this distance and crosses it on a wooden bridge at the 3-mile mark. Unfortunately the pedaling gets slowed in several areas by the so-called "wash board" effect created by motorcycles. The wave-like series of bumps on the trail surface creates a rollercoaster of tiny ups and downs which are not difficult to negotiate but create an extra burden for pedalers.

The trail reaches the center of **Sterling** shortly after this point and intersects **Main St.** (where there is room to park), **Industrial Park Rd.**, and **Rte. 14** within the next half-mile. After leaving Rte. 14, cyclists can enjoy about a half-mile of smooth rolling before the surface gets rougher for the next mile with more berms left from motorcycle usage. Loose sand on the surface also makes the riding more difficult along this part.

Turning due east, the rail bed enters a cut in a small hillside where walls of blasted ledge rise on both sides, then emerges at the site of a missing bridge over **Providence Rd.** Here cyclists must carefully descend a steep, gravelly slope on foot, cross the road, and scramble up the other side. The trail continues to **Spring Lake Rd.** in another half-mile and **Plainfield Pike** (**Rte. 14A**) at the 5.3-mile mark, where there is space for roadside parking.

A smooth surface returns here as the trail enters a scrub oak and pitch pine forest. The trail crosses the Rhode Island state line in another half-mile at the midpoint of a long straightaway where the name changes to the Trestle Trail. It then passes the **Riconn Airport** but trees block any views. The **Nicholas Farm Wildlife Management Area** protects acreage on both sides of the trail including a wetland near **Carbuncle Pond** which allows a view on the left side.

A third of a mile later, the trail crosses a high, wooden bridge over the Moosup River with a good view over the water, crosses gravel-surfaced **Lewis Farm Rd.**, and then climbs a slight incline. Crushed stone forms an even surface along this gradual slope and stone retaining walls line steep bankings along each side.

The trail emerges at the village of **Greene** in Coventry at the 8.1-mile mark and continues with a bermed surface and overgrown conditions. A plaque and a small collection of railroad memorabilia sit beside the railbed in Greene and remind visitors of the village's railroad history.

DRIVING DIRECTIONS:
From I-395 take Exit 89 and follow Rte. 14 east for 1 mile. At the stop sign in Moosup (where Rte. 14 turns left), continue straight into the parking lot in front of the trestle bridge, where the trail starts.
TOILET FACILITIES:
None are provided.
BIKE SHOPS:
Al's Ordinary Bike Shop, 21 Furnace St., Danielson, (860) 774-1660
Central Sports, 137 Norwich Rd., Plainfield, (860) 564-4223
ADDITIONAL INFORMATION:
Connecticut Dept. of Environmental Protection, 79 Elm St., Hartford, CT 06106-5127, Tel. (860) 424-3200,
web: http://dep.state.ct.us
Rhode Island Dept. of Environmental Management,
(401) 222-6800

30
Bluff Point State Park
Groton

length: 5 miles
surface: mostly unpaved with a gravel surface
terrain: small hills

Together with neighboring Haley Farm State Park, Bluff Point offers a variety of biking destinations as well as a range of coastal scenery. Bring your bathing suit and a picnic and plan to spend the day.

BACKGROUND:
This area was settled in the 1600's and remained active farmland for several hundred years. Bluff Point became a popular vacation destination in the 1920's and '30's and hosted a small amusement park, campground, and close to 100 summer cottages until a fierce hurricane in 1938 destroyed much of the area. After nature reclaimed the land, the state began acquiring portions of the peninsula in 1963 and designated the park as a coastal reserve by a special act of the legislature in 1975 to preserve its unique natural and scenic qualities. The park now totals 806 acres.

The nearby Haley Farm State Park property has a long history of owners, including Connecticut's first governor, John Winthrop. From 1869 until 1924, Caleb Haley farmed the land and created its impressive array of stone walls using a so-called stone-puller, a unique device which was drawn by oxen and could manipulate 3-ton boulders into place. Threatened by development proposals in 1963, the property was eventually saved by a local fundraising effort which established this 198-acre park in 1970.

RULES OF THE TRAIL:
Bicyclists are urged to share the trail. Both parks get regular use from walkers so cyclists are asked to ride at safe speeds, yield to hikers and horseback riders, and be

courteous and cautious when passing. Give a friendly call when approaching others from behind to avoid startling them. Bicyclists are also reminded to stay on the trail surface to minimize impacts on the surroundings.

Dogs must be leashed and the park is open only during daylight hours.

ORIENTATION:

Both Bluff Point and Haley Farm have trailhead parking lots which provide direct access to the bike paths. During the summer season, visitors should note that the larger Bluff Point lot is a popular place since it attracts large numbers of swimmers and sunbathers bound for the beach (located at the southern end of the peninsula). It is also the main starting point for mountain bikers who pedal the rougher, narrower trails intersecting the routes described below.

Only one of the trails is marked by signs. Part of Mystic-Groton Bike Route, the trail runs from the Haley Farm State Park trailhead to Midway Oval near the entrance to Bluff Point State Park. Other trails are not marked but offer a good supply of visual landmarks (shown on the map) which include surrounding roads, an active rail line, and numerous coastal views.

TRAIL DESCRIPTIONS:

Starting from the **Bluff Point State Park** trailhead parking lot, the most popular bike path heads south along the shoreline of the **Poquonnock River** to the end of the peninsula. Continue past the trailhead signs on its broad, smooth surface of gravel and fork right at the first intersection. After a short distance, the trail emerges at an open portion of the riverbank where airplanes can be seen approaching Groton-New London Airport on the opposite shore.

The trail returns to the cover of trees, encounters a few small hills, and passes a second intersection at the 1-mile mark. It keeps to flat ground after these hills and then rises on its largest, and final, slope at the 1.4-mile mark,

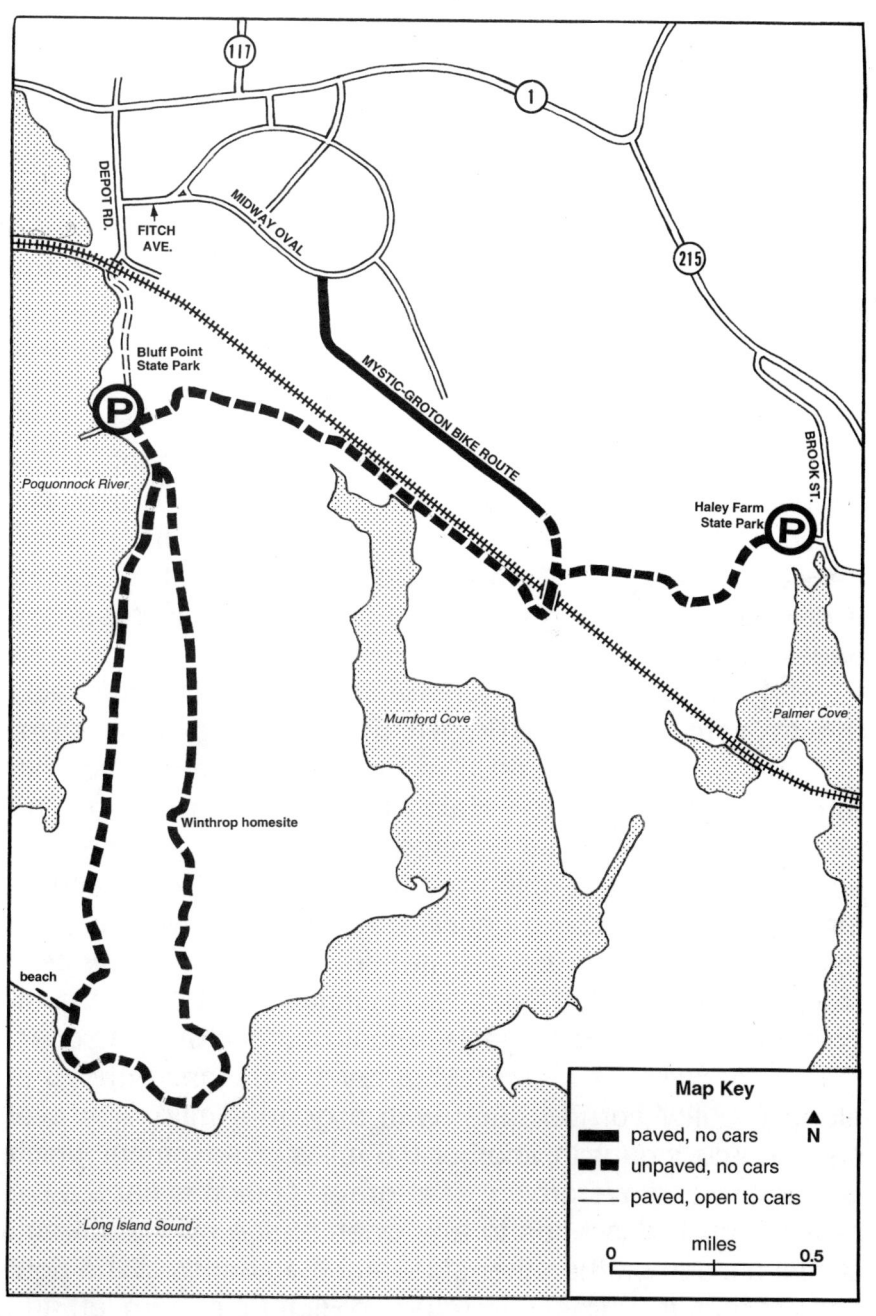

117

1

215

DEPOT RD.

FITCH AVE.

MIDWAY OVAL

MYSTIC-GROTON BIKE ROUTE

BROOK ST.

Bluff Point State Park

P

Poquonnock River

Haley Farm State Park

P

Mumford Cove

Palmer Cove

Winthrop homesite

beach

Long Island Sound

Map Key

N

paved, no cars

unpaved, no cars

paved, open to cars

miles

0   0.5

passes a set of pit toilets at the top, and descends the other side to the **beach** access point at 1.5 miles.

Just past the beach, the trail tops a knoll and captures a great view of **Long Island Sound**. It continues with much hillier, rougher conditions for another mile to the peninsula's highest elevations, where the **Winthrop homesite**, dating from 1700, is marked by a sign in an overgrowing meadow. Mountain bikes are recommended for riding this bumpy trail. An easier means of reaching the Winthrop site is the 0.8-mile trail that forks left from the main trail near the parking lot. It climbs for most of the way with only a few rough spots.

The trail running eastward to **Haley Farm State Park** also leaves from the Bluff Point parking lot. Turn left at the trailhead signs and follow its smooth, flat course past the picnic tables. After a half-mile it merges beside the railroad tracks at a view over **Mumford Cove** and at the 1-mile mark it diverges to the right, climbs a slope, and crosses a pedestrian bridge over the tracks.

Here it enters Haley Farm State Park and intersects the **Mystic-Groton Bike Route**, marked by a sign. Measuring 1.4 miles long, this off-road portion of the bike route runs between the Haley Farm parking lot and the Midway Oval residential neighborhood. Turning to the right and following it for a half-mile to Haley Farm, cyclists curve through the woods on a gentle, quarter-mile downslope and then emerge in the park's meadows where magnificent stone walls define the fields and foundations of the old farm. This portion of the route has a smooth surface of stone dust.

Following it toward **Midway Oval**, the route runs along a utility corridor, first with a quarter-mile of gravel surface and then with another 0.6 miles of pavement which is cracking and overgrown. The gravel portion is flat but the paved portion descends to a wooden bridge over a stream, climbs a slope on the other side, and then bends to the right and reaches the street. To return to Bluff Point, turn left and follow Midway Oval to **Fitch Ave.**, continue straight on Fitch

Ave. to the end, then turn left on **Depot Rd.** and look for the park entrance on the right, dipping underneath the railroad.

DRIVING DIRECTIONS:

To reach Bluff Point State Park from I-95, take Exit 88 and follow Rte. 117 south to Rte. 1. Turn right and follow Rte. 1 west for 0.2 miles, then turn left on Depot Rd. Bear right after a quarter-mile (passing underneath the railroad tracks) and park at the end of the gravel road.

To reach Haley Farm State Park from I-95, take Exit 88 and follow Rte. 117 south to Rte. 1. Turn left and follow Rte. 1 east for 0.9 miles, then turn right (south) on Rte. 215. Continue for a half-mile, turn right on Brook St. and drive for another half-mile, then turn right on Haley Farm La. and park in the lot at the end.

TOILET FACILITIES:

Pit toilets are located at the trailhead parking lots and at the southern end of the Bluff Point peninsula near the beach.

BIKE SHOPS:

Bicycle Barn, 1209 Poquonnock Rd., Groton, (860) 448-2984
Mystic Cycle Center, 42 Williams Ave., Mystic, (860) 572-7433
Terra Cyclery, 154 Williams St., New London, (860) 443-7223
Wayfarer Bicycle, 120 Ocean Ave., New London, (860) 443-8250

ADDITIONAL INFORMATION:

Bluff Point State Park, c/o Fort Griswald State Park, 57 Fort St., Groton, CT 06340, Tel. (860) 445-1729

Appendix

List of Organizations:

Connecticut Bicycle Coalition, 1 Union Place, Hartford,
CT 06103, Tel. (860) 527-5200
web: www.ctbike.org

Connecticut Department of Environmental Protection,
79 Elm St., Hartford, CT 06106-5127, Tel. (860) 424-3200,
web: http://dep.state.ct.us

Connecticut Forest & Park Association, 16 Meriden Rd.,
Rockfall, CT 06481-2961, Tel. (860) 346-8733
web: www.ctwoodlands.org

East Coast Greenway Alliance, 135 Main St., Wakefield,
RI 02879, Tel. (401) 789-4625
web: www.greenway.org

Metropolitan District Commission, P.O. Box 800, Hartford,
CT 06142-0800, Tel. (860) 278-7850
web: www.themdc.com

New England Mountain Bike Association, P.O. Box 2221,
Acton, MA 01720, Tel. (800) 57-NEMBA
web: www.nemba.org

Rails-to-Trails Conservancy, 1100 Seventeenth St. NW,
10'th Floor, Washington, DC 20036, Tel. (202) 331-9696
web: www.railtrails.org

The Trust for Public Land, 383 Orange St., New Haven,
CT 06511, Tel. (203) 777-7367
web: www.tpl.org

Connecticut
Bicycle
Coalition
Advocates for bicycling, walking & sustainable development.

Respect for Cyclists and Their Rights

CBC worked with ConnDOT to produce and market "Share the Road" public service announcements and brochures. In addition, CBC rewrote the chapter of the CT Drivers Manual dealing with bicyclists' rights on the road.

Working for Safer Streets

ConnDOT fails to realize that wider, straighter roads lead to higher speeds and deadly accidents. We will continue to turn up the heat for sound engineering, more funding for bicycle and pedestrian safety, and stepped up enforcement.

Fighting for Pedestrian & Bicycle Improvements Statewide

CBC has convinced some local and state officials that design and engineering can make the difference between vibrant walkable, bikable communities and sterile, lifeless places. We're fighting to make these improvements the norm and not the exception.

GETTING RESULTS for YOU

BECOME A CBC MEMBER TODAY

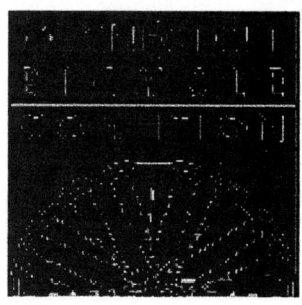

YES! I want to help!

I want to be a part of making Connecticut a better place for bicyclists and pedestrians.

By joining today, you will receive the Citizen Cyclist, our quarterly newsletter which highlights bicycling and transportation news from around the state, along with many other benefits.

You will also receive timely updates about goings-on at the legislature and in your community.

In addition, as a member you receive a **10% discount on gear and apparel** at select businesses.

Print your information clearly on the form below and mail to:
CBC, One Union Place, Hartford, CT 06103

First and Last Name

Street Address (include unit or apt number)

City, State & Zip Code

Home Telephone & E-Mail

MEMBERSHIP CONTRIBUTION

____ **$100**   *Charter Member, receive all of the benefits below, plus a cobalt blue CBC coffee mug.*

____ **$50**   *Supporting Member, receive all benefits below, plus a year's subscription to The Ride magazine.*

____ **$25**   *Basic membership, receive quarterly Citizen Cyclist newsletter, discounts at sponsor shops and area rides.*

Order Form

To receive the following books, send check or money order to:

Active Publications
P.O. Box 1037
Concord, MA 01742-1037

(Massachusetts residents include 5% sales tax.)

___Bike Paths of Connecticut $15.95

___Bike Paths of Massachusetts $15.95

___Mountain Biking Connecticut $15.95

___Mountain Biking Near Boston $15.95

___Mountain Biking New Hampshire $12.95

Name: _____

Address: _____

                _____

Rules of the Bike Path:

1. Keep to the right

2. Pass on the left after audibly signaling

3. Yield to pedestrians

4. Stop at road intersections

5. Be alert

6. Do not obstruct traffic